Railway Stations of Britain

Aberdeen   Ashford   Birmingham   Blackpool   Bolton   Bournemouth
Bradford   Brighton   Bristol   Cambridge   Cardiff   Carlisle
Chester   Clapham Junction   Crewe   Darlington   Derby   Doncaster
Dover   Eastbourne   Edinburgh   Exeter   Gatwick Airport   Glasgow
Harwich   Hereford   Holyhead   Huddersfield   Hull   Inverness
Ipswich   Lancaster   Leeds   Leicester   Lewes   Lincoln   Liverpool   London
Manchester   Margate   Newcastle   Norwich   Nottingham   Perth
Plymouth   Portsmouth   Preston   Ramsgate   Reading   Rugby
Salisbury   Scarborough   Sheffield   Shrewsbury   Southampton
Stafford   Stoke-on-Trent   Wakefield   Warrington   Wigan
Windsor   Wolverhampton   York

Patrick Stephens Limited, part of Thorsons, a division of the Collins Publishing Group, has published authoritative, quality books for enthusiasts for more than twenty years. During that time the company has established a reputation as one of the world's leading publishers of books on aviation, maritime, military, model-making, motor cycling, motoring, motor racing, railway and railway modelling subjects. Readers or authors with suggestions for books they would like to see published are invited to write to: The Editorial Director, Patrick Stephens Limited, Thorsons Publishing Group, Wellingborough, Northants, NN8 2RQ.

RAILWAY STATIONS OF BRITAIN

A guide to 75 important centres

Geoffrey Body MCIT

Patrick Stephens Limited

First published in 1990

British Library Cataloguing
in Publication Data

Body, Geoffrey, *1929-*
   Railway stations of Britain: a guide to
   75 important centres.
   1. Great Britain. Railways. Stations
   I. Title
   385'.314'0941

   ISBN 1-85260-171-X

Key to symbols and abbreviations

B — Bookstall
C — Car parking
I — Information
L — Left luggage
O — Buses
P — Parcels
R — Refreshments
T — Tickets
TC — Travel Centre
U — Underground
X — Taxis

—•— BR passenger line and open station
••••••• BR line underground
+++++++ BR freight line
— o — Closed line and station
—·—·—·— Non-BR line
→ ← Tunnel
⊠ Signal Box
× × Level Crossing
× ×

NB On outline system maps (overleaf),
   open BR lines are shown +++++++

Patrick Stephens Limited is part of the
Thorsons Publishing Group,
Wellingborough, Northamptonshire
NN8 2RQ, England.

Typeset by Harper Phototypesetters Ltd
Northampton England.
Printed in Great Britain by
Butler & Tanner, Frome, Somerset

10 9 8 7 6 5 4 3 2 1

INTRODUCTION

The origins of joining and alighting points for public carriers goes right back to stagecoach days when operators made stopping or staging posts out of convenient inns so that their passengers could wait in comfort or take refreshments during a break in the journey. The early railways carried on the practice, although something better was usually provided at each end of the route, often as much to convince the influential of the respectability of the enterprise as for the comfort of the new breed of travellers. The 1830 Liverpool & Manchester Railway, for example, provided quite reasonable termini at Crown Street, Liverpool and Liverpool Road, Manchester, but the intermediate stations tended to be where turnpike roads were crossed and an innkeeper could act both as host and as booking agent.

As railways came to serve points where no inn existed and as trains became longer, the need for bigger and more frequent stations as we know them became apparent, with platforms, an office and a signalman's cabin. Railway growth was such that the first generation of stations often proved inadequate and those that followed were purpose-built stopping points, often of considerable size and style. Inns continued to have a role at smaller stations while the larger ones normally had a companion hotel. Examples of public houses booking tickets and hotels having a dedicated entrance or conveyance for rail passengers even lingered on into the BR era.

The first main stations were often single platform affairs, but the generation that replaced them produced more complex and often quite extravagant structures. The good buildings of the early years, like those of the Newcastle & Berwick Railway, were followed by some lavish ones, like York or the Midland's complex of station and hotel at St Pancras. Not only did these new stations have a great deal of variety and style but they were also places of high operational interest. Up to half a dozen individual railways might use a station like York, and each had its own individual locomotives, rolling stock, livery and working practices. At Cambridge, for example, the Great Eastern, Great Northern, Midland and London & North Western companies all worked into the station and the locomotive mixture might range from an immaculate engine on a royal train to Wolferton to a grubby LNWR 'Cauliflower' arriving in the goods yard.

Nationalization of the railway system inevitably produced a tendency towards uniformity, but the BR giant has been generally careful of its heritage. Coupled with advances in technology, this has meant that modern stations still hold much of interest and excitement. The aim of this book has been to select and portray those with the most to offer, not just the largest or the busiest, nor even the oldest or the most important architecturally, but something of an amalgam of these considerations which might be labelled 'character'.

For each of the 75 centres included in this book the entry presents an outline area map to clarify the surroundings and an overall station diagram to show the track layout and principal public facilities. The data panel then summarizes the origins, location, routes, services and facilities of the station, with details of features considered to be of special interest. This outline picture is amplified in the text section which describes the history and salient features of each location.

A fairly standard format has been used throughout the book but has not been allowed to get in the way of clarity and readability. For the train services, diagrams and other data, a datum year of 1988 has been taken as this affords both a good basis for comparing back to the stable year of 1938 or forward to the many changes now afoot, not least the current electrification of the East Coast Main Line.

The author gratefully acknowledges the assistance of British Rail in connection with this work. Its compilation has entailed visiting all the stations featured and this has been supplemented by reference to a considerable volume of literature on stations. Those wishing to know more will find the David & Charles publications, especially the 'Regional History of the Railways of Great Britain' series, and Patrick Stephens' 'Field Guides' to the BR regions especially helpful. The maps and diagrams in the book were drawn by Ian G. Body.

Outline Map of the BR System Showing Main Stations

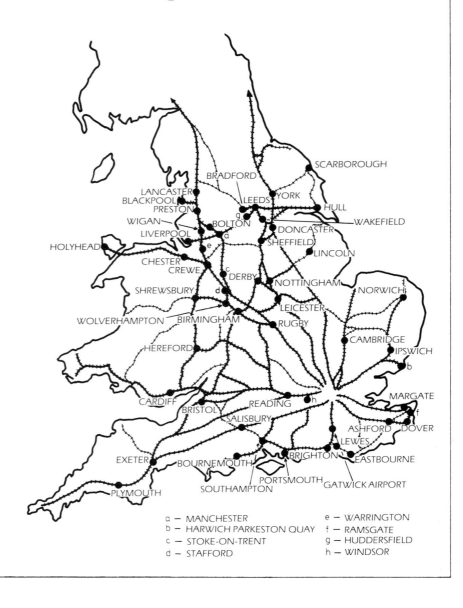

SCARBOROUGH
BRADFORD
LANCASTER
BLACKPOOL
PRESTON
LEEDS
YORK
HULL
WIGAN
BOLTON
g
WAKEFIELD
LIVERPOOL
DONCASTER
HOLYHEAD
e
a
SHEFFIELD
CHESTER
LINCOLN
CREWE
c
DERBY
SHREWSBURY
d
NOTTINGHAM
NORWICH
WOLVERHAMPTON
BIRMINGHAM
LEICESTER
RUGBY
HEREFORD
CAMBRIDGE
IPSWICH
b
MARGATE
CARDIFF
READING
h
BRISTOL
SALISBURY
ASHFORD
DOVER
LEWES
f
EXETER
BOURNEMOUTH
BRIGHTON
EASTBOURNE
PLYMOUTH
PORTSMOUTH
SOUTHAMPTON
GATWICK AIRPORT

a — MANCHESTER   e — WARRINGTON
b — HARWICH PARKESTON QUAY   f — RAMSGATE
c — STOKE-ON-TRENT   g — HUDDERSFIELD
d — STAFFORD   h — WINDSOR

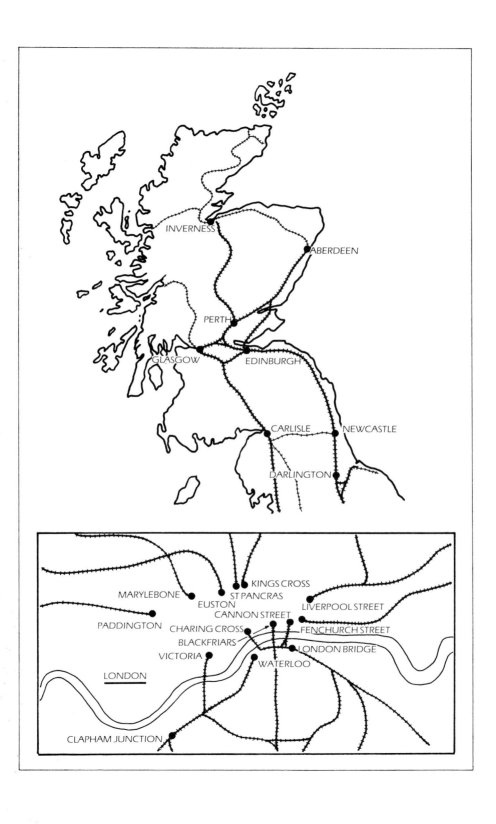

INVERNESS

ABERDEEN

PERTH

GLASGOW

EDINBURGH

CARLISLE

NEWCASTLE

DARLINGTON

MARYLEBONE

KINGS CROSS

ST PANCRAS

EUSTON

LIVERPOOL STREET

CANNON STREET

PADDINGTON

CHARING CROSS

FENCHURCH STREET

BLACKFRIARS

VICTORIA

LONDON BRIDGE

WATERLOO

LONDON

CLAPHAM JUNCTION

ABERDEEN JOINT STATION

Origins: opened 1867, Caledonian and Great North of Scotland Railways; rebuilt 1913-16 and refurbished by BR.
Location: extension of East Coast Main Line and junction with line to Inverness. 524 miles from King's Cross.
Main routes: ECML, Edinburgh-Dundee-Aberdeen and Glasgow-Perth-Dundee-Aberdeen.
Other routes: Aberdeen-Inverness.
Services: InterCity services to King's Cross, including sleepers, the 'Flying Scotsman' and the 'Aberdonian'; also the 'Clansman' and the 'Night Aberdonian' to Euston and the 'Devon Scot' to Plymouth. Scotrail expresses to Glasgow and Edinburgh, and local service on Inverness line. 67 trains daily in 1988. Fastest service to London (King's Cross) 7 hours 13 minutes (72.6 mph), 1938 9 hours 45 minutes (53.7 mph).
Platforms: 7, including 5 bays.
Facilities: Travel Centre, refreshments, bookstall, parcels and left luggage, parking, car hire, taxis, bus station nearby.
Of special interest: GNofSR war memorial, Guild Street offices, goods shed and depot, Station Hotel, fuelling plant and washer on Down side.

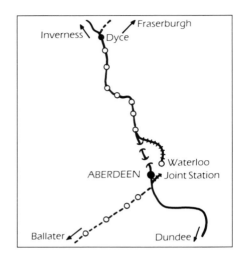

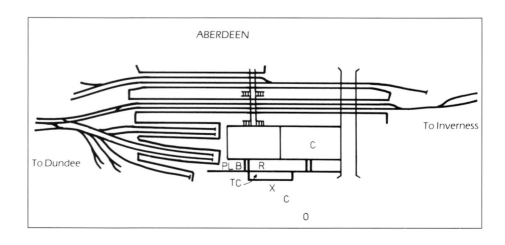

Ahead, in Guild Street Aberdeen, stands the GNofSR Station Hotel, while the present station is on the left.

The approach to Aberdeen along the North Sea coast from Stonehaven gives an excellent view of the pleasant skyline of the Granite City. The BR station then matches that initial impression, having been attractively modernized with a light, airy concourse and provided with a well-equipped Travel Centre along the main frontage. Its situation is convenient for city and docks and there is a bus station nearby.

The Aberdeen Railway reached Aberdeen from the south in 1850 and was to have been amalgamated with the Great North of Scotland concern. But this was not to be, and when the GNofSR Huntley-Kittybrewster line was extended to Aberdeen in 1855 it was to a separate station at Waterloo Quay. Passenger traffic began in 1856, but another 11 years were to pass before a joint station was built on the former Guild Street site. Then, the Caledonian Railway, as successors to the Aberdeen and Scottish North Eastern companies, partnered the GNofSR in a Guild Street combination of terminal and through station, the two partners rebuilding the location in 1913-16.

A double span bridge carries the cobbles of Guild Street over the station's through lines and their canopies. The frontage then runs at right angles to the street and since 1985 has accommodated a Travel Centre beneath the upper works of seven sections separated by double pilasters. A marbled passageway then leads to the sizeable concourse with its ribbed and braced ridge roof. A modern indicator stands in front of the double footbridge staircase which now leads only to platform 7, the other side of the island and the outer through platform being out of use. Beyond the south end screens of the concourse are five curved bay platforms; at the north end there is a car park.

The Aberdeen Travel Centre accommodates the GNofSR war memorial previously housed in the company's offices at 80 Guild Street. That company also owned the Station Hotel while another building nearby is the goods shed, still displaying a traditional interior. The goods yard remains active and there are locomotive fuelling facilities on the Down side of the station.

ASHFORD

Origins: first station opened 1842, South Eastern Railway; rebuilt by BR 1961-63.

Location: former SER Dover main line, junction with Maidstone, Hastings and Ramsgate lines. 56 miles from Charing Cross.

Main routes: Victoria-Ashford and Ramsgate/Margate via Maidstone East, and Charing Cross-Dover/Margate.

Other routes: Ashford-Hastings/Bexhill-on-Sea.

Services: main line electric trains Charing Cross-Dover/Margate separating at Ashford. Charing Cross-Ashford and Victoria-Maidstone East-Ashford (and Ramsgate/Margate) services; also to Hastings/Bexhill-on-Sea. 210 trains daily in 1988. Fastest service to London 1 hour (56 mph), 1938 1 hour 14 minutes (45.4 mph).

Platforms: 4.

Facilities: tickets and information, refreshments, bookstall, parcels, left luggage, parking, taxis, local buses.

Of special interest: traffic working, including freight; former works area, Chart Leacon depot.

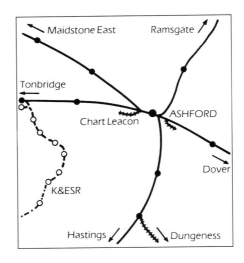

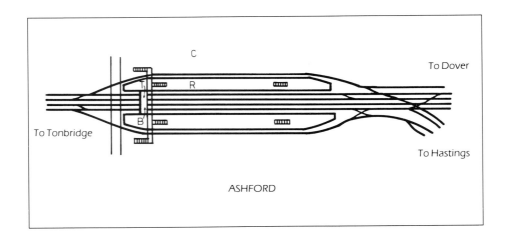

ASHFORD

A four-car set for Charing Cross has just completed a Down journey and waits to return.

For a major junction location with five radiating routes, Ashford deals with its sizeable traffic load in a very unassuming manner. Compared with the 10 minutes required in steam days, Ashford regularly unites and separates the Dover and Margate portions of Charing Cross trains in an unruffled 3 minutes. Its other Dover trains, plus those to Hastings and Ashford's own service to Charing Cross, are handled with a similar lack of fuss at its modern, functional four-platform station.

The original main line of the South Eastern Railway reached Ashford on 1 December 1842, pushed on to Folkestone in the following year and achieved its Dover target in 1844. Just three years later the growing South Eastern opened a locomotive works east of the station and subsequently added a wagon works as well, using sites adjoining the 1846 route to Margate. The Ashford locomotive works closed in 1962 and the BREL depot 22 years later, but the tradition of traction and stock maintenance is carried on at Chart Leacon depot west of the station. Built on a former swamp at the time of the Kent Coast electrification, Chart Leacon repairs and

overhauls a large volume of SR suburban rolling stock as well as doing locomotive and multiple unit work.

Rebuilt and enlarged in the early 1900s and rebuilt again in the 1960s, Ashford station is located in Beaver Road, about ¼ mile from the shopping centre. Access is from a bridge which houses the ticket and information office, stairs then leading to the two island platforms. There, brick buildings house the station administration and a modern overall canopy provides protection from the elements. Between the platforms run the Up and Down Main lines plus Up and Down Platform lines, with platform loops passing outside the two islands.

The West Yard at Ashford, located where the Maidstone East route joins the main line, was the site of the London, Chatham & Dover Railway terminus until 1899. The lines to Hythe and New Romney have also closed, as have the works, but apart from these contractions Ashford continues to play a vital role in the modern railway age. It may even get an international station with the opening of the Channel Tunnel.

BIRMINGHAM NEW STREET SNOW HILL

LNWR/LMS/LMR
GWR/GWR/LMR

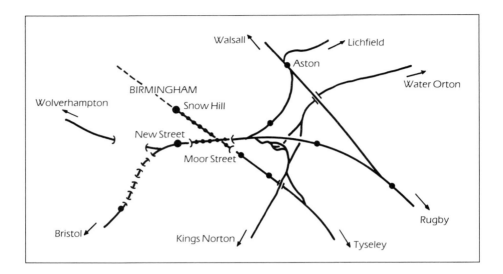

Origins: New Street opened 1854, London & North Western Railway, rebuilt by BR and reopened 1967-68. Snow Hill opened 1852, Great Western Railway; closed 1972, reopened 1987.

Location: New Street is on the original West Coast Main Line route, 115¼ miles from Euston, and a major interchange point with other routes, including the NE/SW main line. Snow Hill is the terminus for Leamington and Stratford trains on the former GWR route, Moor Street lying on this route and Birmingham International on the main line from Coventry.

Main routes: West Coast Main Line electrically-hauled InterCity services Euston/Birmingham-North West/Scotland. Intensive electric service Wolverhampton/Birmingham-Euston. South and South West to West and East Coast Main Lines and Manchester/Liverpool. Cross-country routes to Lincolnshire via Newark and East Anglia via Peterborough. Also services via Shrewsbury, via Oxford to Paddington and to Cardiff.

Other routes: Midline local routes in conjunction with West Midland PTA, eg Lichfield-Redditch, New Street-Walsall and Snow Hill-Leamington/Stratford; intensive emu service to Coventry, Rugby and south thereof. Other services on Worcester/Hereford, Leicester/Nottingham and Stoke/Manchester lines.

Services: on the main line, electric services link New Street with Coventry and Euston (via Birmingham International) to the south, and to Manchester/Liverpool and Glasgow/Edinburgh to the north. The 'Clansman' and the Plymouth-Scotland sleeper call, as do other services via Bristol and Reading and on via Derby or Crewe, including the 'Armada', 'Devonian', 'Cornishman', 'Northumbrian' and the 'Devon', 'Wessex', and 'Sussex' and 'Cornish' 'Scots'. Emu services operate to Stoke-on-Trent and Manchester, and Sprinters on the cross-country routes to Norwich/Cambridge via Peterborough, to Lincoln/Cleethorpes via Newark and via Wolverhampton to

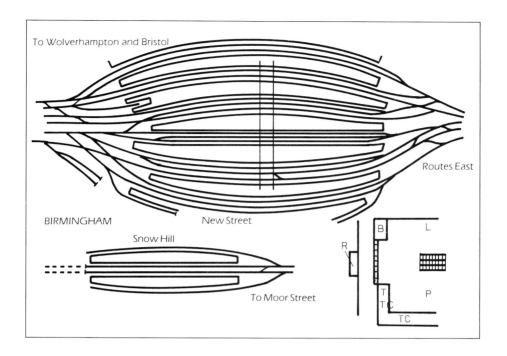

To Wolverhampton and Bristol

Routes East

BIRMINGHAM New Street

Snow Hill

To Moor Street

Shrewsbury/Chester. Commuter/local services, in conjunction with the West Midlands PTA, on the non-electrified lines south (to Redditch and Stourbridge/Worcester/Great Malvern/Hereford), and on the routes north to Lichfield and Walsall. Local services from Snow Hill via Moor Street out as far as Leamington and Stratford, plus Oxford-Paddington services from New Street. 873 trains daily from New Street in 1988, 222 from Birmingham International and 143 from Snow Hill and Moor Street. Fastest service to London 1 hour 28 minutes (78.6 mph), 1938 1 hour 55 minutes (60.1 mph).

Platforms: 12.

Facilities: New Street — ticket office, Travel Centre and European Travel Centre, refreshments, bookstall, parcels, left luggage, parking nearby, taxis, local buses. Snow Hill — bookstall and local buses. Both adjacent to main shopping areas.

Of special interest: New Street train operations, Curzon Street buildings, former Moor Street terminus, new Snow Hill development, Museum of Science & Industry in Newhall Street

As might be expected, the principal city of the Midlands is also an important rail centre where major InterCity routes intersect and where thousands of commuters make their daily journeys on the trains which BR operates on behalf of the West Midlands PTE. The main station is New Street which handles 80 per cent of the daily total of services including the long-distance trains from Euston to the North, the well-used services from the South and South West to Scotland, Newcastle and Manchester/Liverpool and the east-west services to East Anglia and through Central Wales. Snow Hill and Moor Street deal with trains out to Stratford-upon-Avon and Leamington Spa while Birmingham International, 8½ miles out on the Coventry line, is busy with airport and National Exhibition Centre traffic.

All this began with a very modest Vauxhall train shed which the Grand

Birmingham New Street looks dark and cavernous beneath the vast shopping centre development rising above it.

Junction Railway provided for its trains to the north in 1837. It was followed in 1838 by the London & Birmingham Railway's Curzon Street for which Philip Hardwick provided a rectangular building decorated by Ionic columns and approached through ornamental iron gates. The two-platform station was connected to its GJR neighbour to allow through services between London and the North West. The Birmingham & Derby Junction Railway and the Birmingham & Gloucester Railway, destined to contribute to the creation of the Midland Railway and today's North East/South West route, initially used a terminus at Lawley Street but then transferred to the L&B station and added to the congestion which, together with an inconvenient location, was to lead to its replacement by New Street. Both Lawley Street and Curzon Street continued as goods depots and the former, after a fallow period following the 1968 closure, became a local authority centre for community support groups.

Although the LNWR's Trent Valley cut-off line took some of the London traffic away from Birmingham, this was more than offset by the growth in its own railway activity, which included the arrival of

A dmu set emerges from the reopened Snow Hill Tunnel and draws into Birmingham Moor Street.

The tracks of the reopened Snow Hill station are just visible beneath the modern development above it.

the Great Western Railway. Initial distrust between the Grand Junction and London & Birmingham companies virtually invited GWR involvement. When it came it was to produce a new main line to London via Oxford and, from the 1852 opening of the Birmingham & Oxford Railway, a new Birmingham station which was later to be called Snow Hill. Although Snow Hill was to close after 120 years of operational service, it has now been reopened under a West Midlands PTA initiative and is again dealing with passengers to and from the former GWR main line.

The New Street station which replaced Curzon Street became fully operational from 1 June 1854 and in 1885 was given separate platforms for its Midland Railway services. It later became a joint station, with the LNWR and MR then handing it over to the LMS to manage the 14 platforms crowded beneath a vast roof and spanned by a long footbridge which preserved an old right of way. This old New Street, no great shakes as stations go, was replaced in a major scheme linked with BR's electrification of the area. Its 12 through platforms now lie beneath a vast shopping and office complex and are reached by triple escalators. These lead to a large circulating area embracing the ticketing, information and other services, with access to the trains then being from

a long passageway which accommodates further facilities. The station is well laid out and operated, but very functional.

In contrast to New Street, the other Birmingham stations are quite pleasant. Birmingham International is a straight-forward affair of two island platforms with the Magalev train for airport users on one side and the National Exhibition Centre facilities on the other. Moor Street now consists of two platforms with canopies, a modern ticket office and ramp access, all in colourful materials. From 28 September 1987 it took over from the old four-platform ex-GWR station nearby and gave up its terminal status to become a through station on the new line into Snow Hill.

After rebuilding between 1909 and 1912, the substantial through station at Snow Hill was closed on 6 March 1972 and demolished five years later. Now it has come to life again under a scheme funded by the West Midlands PTA, with Government and EEC support, which provided for the reopening of the 596-yard tunnel from Moor Street. The station's two island platforms are part of an impressive development of the whole Colmore Row area which has an office block and car park complex built over the site and provides covered walkway access to the small concourse that precedes the stairs and lifts to the platforms.

BLACKPOOL NORTH SOUTH

LYR&LNWR/LMS/LMS
LYR&LNWR/LMS/LMS

Origins: Blackpool North opened 1846, Preston & Wyre Railway, rebuilt by BR. Blackpool South opened 1863, Lancashire & Yorkshire and London & North Western Joint.

Location: Blackpool North is the terminus of the line from Preston. 226½ miles from Euston. Blackpool South is the terminus of a second line from Preston, via Lytham.

Main routes: Blackpool North to Manchester Victoria, Leeds/York, East Anglia, Liverpool and Euston.

Other routes: Blackpool South-Preston/Colne.

Services: InterCity services to Euston, cross-Pennine service via Burnley, trains to East Anglia via Nottingham, to Liverpool, and interval service to Manchester Victoria. The 'Loreley' to and from Parkeston Quay. Service to Preston/Colne from Blackpool South. Blackpool North 108 trains daily in 1988, 30 from South. Fastest service to London 3 hours 35 minutes (63.3 mph), 1938 4 hours 25 minutes (51.9 mph).

Platforms: North — 8; South — 1.

Facilities: North — tickets and information, refreshments, parcels, left luggage, car park, taxis, local buses

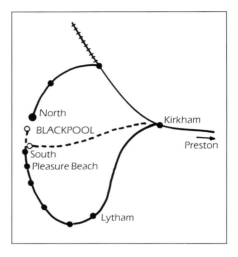

nearby.

Of special interest: residue of once-extensive stabling and servicing areas, Blackpool Coastal Tramway promenade route (Starr Gate-Talbot Square-Fleetwood).

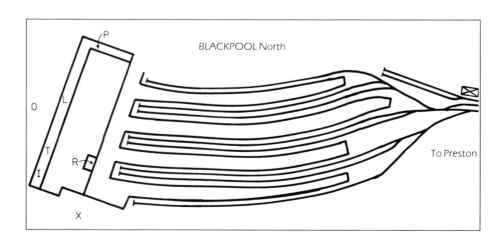

Just behind the seafront and shopping centre stands the 1974 eight-platform station at Blackpool North.

Blackpool North, the town's main station, uses the site of the first railway arrival, the Preston & Wyre Railway. That was back in 1846 when a branch from the Fleetwood line at Poulton was opened on 29 April to serve the seaside village that was eventually to become the leisure metropolis of the North West. A second railway reached Blackpool from Lytham on 6 April 1863, anticipating a period of development at the resort as it began to compete with Southport for the Wakes Week traffic of the mill towns. The third route, a direct line from Kirkham, increased still further the numbers of holidaymakers and daytrippers from 30 May 1903.

The railway approach from the south used a large terminus known as Blackpool Central, trains from Poulton running into another at Talbot Road (later Blackpool North), and those on the 1903 line using Waterloo Road, effectively today's Blackpool South. The volume of summer Saturday traffic necessitated extensive carriage sidings, two loco sheds and other support facilities. From 1895 visitors flocked to see the Blackpool Tower, with even more arriving after the establishment of the 'Illuminations' spectacle in the 1920s. The LYR introduced a system of travel regulation as early as 1919 in an attempt to cope with the massive numbers.

The BR rationalization era brought about the closure of Central station on 2 November 1964, the route via Lytham now terminating at the single platform of Blackpool South. This is preceded by another single platform at Blackpool

Pleasure Beach. The direct route from Kirkham then closed just over a year later, with the London services being concentrated on Blackpool North at the beginning of the 1970s and a new station being provided there in 1974. This made use of the former excursion platforms of the 1846 station, leaving the six shorter platforms for parking and development areas. The surviving eight platforms are backed by a modern, rectangular facilities block in brick with a glazed roof section elevated on concrete angle beams. The shops and seafront are not far away and Britain's only surviving municipal tramway operates along the promenade.

A Sprinter unit stands in the surviving single platform at Blackpool South, ready for its next working to Preston.

BOLTON TRINITY STREET

Origins: opened 1838, Manchester, Bolton & Bury Canal Navigation & Railway. Rebuilt 1903, Lancashire & Yorkshire Railway; new entrance 1987, BR and Greater Manchester PTE.

Location: junction of Manchester-Blackburn and Manchester-Preston/Southport lines. 10¾ miles from Manchester (Victoria).

Main routes: Manchester (Victoria)-Bolton-Blackpool and Manchester-Bolton-Southport. Blackpool-East Anglia.

Other routes: Manchester (Victoria)-Bolton, and Manchester-Bolton-Blackburn.

Services: InterCity trains to Scotland, fast Preston/Blackpool and Manchester services, plus through Barrow-in-Furness, Sheffield/Derby and Blackburn-Bolton-Ipswich/Cambridge/Parkeston Quay Sprinters, including the 'Loreley'. Blackburn-Bolton-Manchester and Kirkby/Southport-Wigan-Bolton-Manchester trains. 205 trains daily in 1988. Fastest service to Manchester 15 minutes (43 mph), 1938 17 minutes (37.9 mph).

Platforms: 3.

Facilities: ticket office and travel

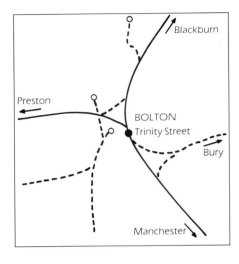

centre, refreshments, bookstall, parcels and left luggage, taxis, bus interchange adjacent.

Of special interest: engraved windows of platform buildings; 'Telegraph Office' and 'Ladies' 1st and 2nd Class Waiting Room'. Also platform 3 model of SS *King Orry* with showcase lettered 'Express train and steamer services to the Isle of Man'.

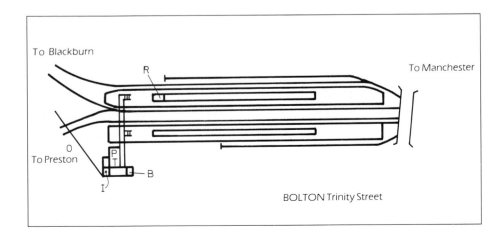

Bolton was part of the great railway pioneering which took place in Lancashire and which culminated in the opening of the world's first inter-city line, that of the Liverpool & Manchester Railway, in 1830. George Stephenson had by then already built the 7¾-mile Bolton & Leigh Railway, a tramroad which was worked by stationary engines and horses when it commenced operation in 1828. By 1831 the B&L was connected to the Liverpool & Manchester route and was using Stephenson locomotives to haul trains to and from a Bolton terminus at Great Moor Street. More direct routes between Great Moor Street and Manchester came into use in 1864 and 1875, when the station was rebuilt. It was closed to passengers on 29 March 1954, apart from some Wakes Week traffic.

The first station on the Trinity Street site was that of the Manchester, Bolton & Bury Canal Navigation & Railway which opened to a terminus there on 29 May 1838. The route was extended by the Bolton & Preston Railway in 1843 and Bolton grew steadily in railway importance as further routes developed via Wigan, Blackburn and Bury, plus a branch to Astley Bridge. The Lancashire & Yorkshire Railway's four major routes from Bolton Trinity Street rather eclipsed the activities of its LNWR rival at Great Moor Street, although the latter retained good links with Manchester, Liverpool and Warrington.

Trinity Street station was rebuilt in 1903-4 in red brick with domed cupolas and a clock tower, but its buildings have now been demolished and replaced by a new station access 100 yards away in Newport Street. There, modern buildings funded by BR and the Greater Manchester PTA and adjoining a bus interchange depot were opened on 8 March 1987. They lead by footbridge to two island platforms which have buildings in dark and light glazed bricks, the main ones on the Down side rising in plainer form above the canopy. The Down side bays are now filled in and only a terminating parcels line uses the outer face there. Preston line trains use the inner platform faces and those on the Blackburn line the two sides of the Up island, No 3 platform line being bi-directional.

A two-car Class 142 set bound for Southport stands at Bolton, near the track remnants of the through lines.

BOURNEMOUTH CENTRAL

Origins: opened 1885, London & South Western Railway.

Location: major station on former LSWR main line to Weymouth. 108 miles from Waterloo.

Main routes: Weymouth/Poole-Waterloo.

Other routes: none.

Services: Wessex Electrics Weymouth/Poole-Bournemouth-Waterloo, including the 'Royal Wessex'. Also the 'Wessex Scot' to Glasgow/Edinburgh, the 'Northumbrian' to Newcastle, and Manchester/Liverpool services via Reading and Birmingham. Local Wareham-Southampton trains. 127 trains daily in 1988. Fastest service to London 1 hour 36 minutes (67.5 mph), 1938 1 hour 59 minutes (54.8 mph).

Platforms: 3.

Facilities: ticket and information offices, refreshments and small bookstall, parcels, left luggage, parking, taxis, local buses pass, coach station nearby.

Of special interest: main station block and traditional signal box.

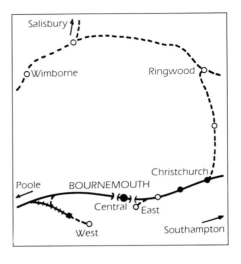

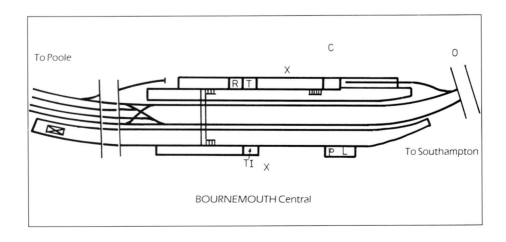

BOURNEMOUTH Central

An Up train standing in Bournemouth's 1885 station which retains most of its massive roof section.

Not large enough then to figure in the route planning of the 1847 Southampton & Dorchester Railway, Bournemouth did not get its own railway connection until 14 March 1870 when the Ringwood-Christchurch line was extended to a point just east of the present station. Four years later a line was opened from Poole to Bournemouth West, prompting plans for a more direct approach from the Southampton direction and a link line between the two Bournemouth stations.

The original Bournemouth East station was replaced by the present one from 20 July 1885 and from 6 March of the following year the direct route from Brockenhurst and on through the town to a junction with the Poole line came into service. In 1899 Bournemouth East became Bournemouth Central. Bournemouth West, mainly used for a service over the S&D line to Brockenhurst and one to Wimborne, was closed in 1965 and its approaches used to provide a carriage servicing depot for the electric services which began a year later.

The new station built by the LSWR in 1885 remains in use today, although with part of the overall roof removed and with the central through lines taken up. It consists, essentially, of two long platforms with exceptionally high outer walls linked by 12 latticed roof support members, themselves supported by huge ornate brackets rising from solid buttresses. The Up side has a matching extension from the main facade, including the ticket office inscribed 1885, and a single-storey arcade backing the enclosed, but now unused, No 1 bay. There are subway and footbridge links from the main Up platform (No 2) to the Down side (No 3), which is extended at the country end to form No 4 where the signal box is located beyond a trunk road overbridge. No 4 platform was used for local Down services prior to the introduction of the Wessex Electric through services from May 1988.

Bournemouth station is reached via access roads from Holdenhurst Road, along which local buses cover the ¾-mile distance to the town centre and main beach area. The high walls in warm red brick make it an imposing location, contrasting with the modern design of an adjacent supermarket.

BRADFORD INTERCHANGE FORSTER SQUARE

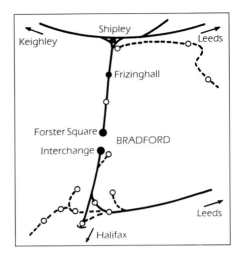

Origins: Interchange opened by BR/West Yorkshire PTE 1977 in former LYR Exchange station area. Forster Square opened 1846, Leeds & Bradford Railway; rebuilt 1890 by MR.

Location: Interchange is the Bradford terminus for Leeds and Manchester line trains, 195½ miles from King's Cross. Forster Square deals with the routes via Shipley and is 211¼ miles from St Pancras.

Main routes: Interchange — Scarborough-Manchester and York-Blackpool. Forster Square — Leeds-Morecambe/Carlisle.

Other routes: Interchange — York-Halifax and Bradford-Leeds. Forster Square — to Keighley/Skipton and Ilkley branch.

Services: InterCity services to King's Cross and St Pancras, including the 'Bradford Executive', plus services over the routes shown above. 131 trains daily from Interchange in 1988, 69 from Forster Square. Fastest service to London 2 hours 49 minutes (69.3 mph), 1938 3 hours 5 minutes (63.5 mph).

Platforms: Interchange — 4, Forster Square — 2.

Facilities: tickets, parking, taxis and local buses at both; information, refreshments, bookstall, parcels and left luggage at Interchange.

Of special interest: the purpose-built Interchange complex, Midland Hotel, MR spandrels of Forster Square overbridge.

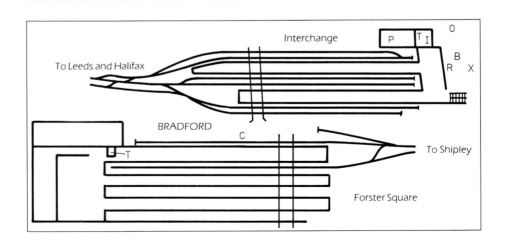

Bradford Interchange station is to the right, the parcels office and Victoria Hotel ahead, and the bus/coach station to the left.

There have been several schemes to link the two Bradford stations but they remain separate, although not far apart and both close to the city centre. The senior of the two locations is Forster Square, opened on 1 July 1846 when the trains of the Leeds & Bradford Railway began linking those two cities via Shipley and the valley of the River Aire. It increased in stature as the extension west from Shipley turned into a Midland Railway main line which was to carry its Scottish expresses. The original L&B Market Street location was then rebuilt as Forster Square in 1890. With six platforms linked by an arcade to the frontage with its tall chimneys and small tower, the once-busy Forster Square was simplified in the mid-1970s and now has only two tracks in use. However, it has regained some InterCity services on an experimental basis and is being rescued from its former run-down state.

The Lancashire & Yorkshire gave Bradford its second station, later called Exchange, on 9 May 1850, with the Great Northern adding Adolphus Street in 1855 but increasingly using Exchange from 1867. The latter was completely rebuilt in 1888 and then lasted until 1973 when it was demoted to a car parking site. However, part of the location was used for the present Interchange station which handles trains on the Leeds and Manchester routes.

At Interchange an escalator leads from the ground floor concourse and the adjoining bus and coach depot to the raised BR/Metro station. This consists of ticket and information offices and four platforms plus parcels and stabling lines.

The two Bradford stations are in considerable contrast, Interchange simple and modern and Forster Square traditional and under-utilized. The latter has six platforms under an overall roof, but only two are in use. Alongside Forster Square is the Midland Hotel which was also part of the remodelling of the square at the end of the 1880s and is the work of Charles Trubshaw. It is in a somewhat flamboyant style and carries a plaque recording that Sir Henry Irving died there in October 1905.

A lone unit stands at the principal operational platform at Bradford Forster Square in 1988. Note the bridge supports.

BRIGHTON

Origins: opened 1840-41, London & Brighton Railway, architect David Mocatta; new roof and other alterations 1882-83.

Location: southern terminus of ex-LB&SCR main line from Victoria and of coastal routes from Portsmouth and Eastbourne. 51 miles from Victoria.

Main routes: Brighton-Redhill-Victoria/Bedford, Brighton-Portsmouth Harbour, Brighton-Hastings and Brighton-NW/Scotland via Reading.

Other routes: Brighton-Worthing/Littlehampton, Brighton-Seaford.

Services: London & South East main line electrics to Victoria/London Bridge and via Thameslink route to Bedford; Manchester/Liverpool service and the 'Sussex Scot' to Glasgow/Edinburgh. Sprinter links with Bristol and Cardiff. Coast Line electrics west to Worthing/Littlehampton/Portsmouth and east to Seaford/Eastbourne/Hastings. 361 trains daily in 1988. Fastest service to London 51 minutes (60 mph), 1938 1 hour (51 mph).

Platforms: 8.

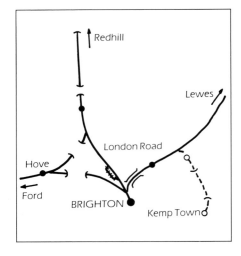

Facilities: Travel Centre, ticket office, refreshments, bookstall, parcels and left luggage, parking, car hire, taxis and local buses.

Of special interest: LB&SCR clock, John Saxby commemorative plaque, London Road Viaduct, Volks Electric Railway on seafront.

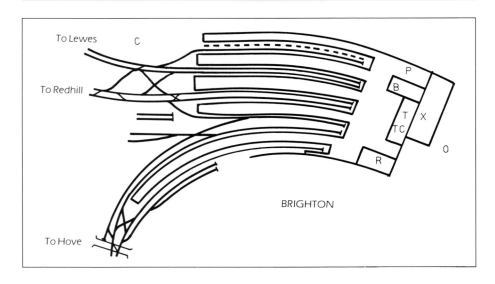

Brighton station with the original frontage between the 1882-83 additions. Note the ornamental ironwork.

The impressive Brighton terminus of the former London, Brighton & South Coast Railway accommodates three busy modern rail routes, the main line from London and the coastal routes from east and west of the resort. The goods yard area east of the station is now used for car parking but the railway works tradition is kept alive by the maintenance depot on the Up side of the main line. The station itself, with two dramatic roof spans covering its surviving eight platforms, is approached from the east over the 27 arches of London Road Viaduct which links the Lewes line and its traditional London Road station with the Brighton terminus.

Architect David Mocatta and engineer John Urpeth Rastrick created the viaduct for the 1846 Lewes line, the same partnership having produced the station just over five years earlier. The main line had reached Brighton in 1841, following the opening of the Worthing line on 11 May of the previous year, and the Mocatta/Rastrick partnership had produced a station worthy of the Regency resort. From 1869 it was

also to handle trains on the branch round to Thomas Read Kemp's development at Kemp Town.

Approaching from Queens Road, the station seems dominated by the large *porte-cochère* which was added in a period of alterations in 1882-83. Above its decorated iron columns the upper storey and ornate clock gable of the Mocatta frontage remain uncluttered. The LB&SCR Board used to meet here, in front of the two great roof spans which replaced Rastrick's originals in 1882-83 and look out over the town to the sea-front beyond.

A modern Travel Centre and ticket office have replaced Brighton's traditional booking hall but once out on the concourse there is a reminder of the past in the ornate four-sided LB&SCR clock which hangs near the modern train indicator. Ahead, on the west side, a long platform curves beneath the high Terminus Road retaining wall to finish up pointing towards Hove Tunnel. On the east side the wooden platform 9 has been abandoned as the layout permits eastbound trains to use four lines in the central portion of the station.

BRISTOL TEMPLE MEADS

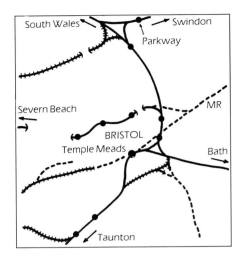

Origins: opened 1878, Great Western Railway with MR, architect Sir Matthew Digby Wyatt.

Location: original GWR main line, junction with Birmingham route. 118½ miles from Paddington.

Main routes: Weston-super-Mare/Bristol-Paddington; South West-North East/North West/Scotland via Birmingham; Cardiff-Bristol-Southampton-Portsmouth.

Other routes: to Weymouth, Severn Beach and Weston/Taunton.

Services: InterCity HSTs to Paddington, including the 'Brunel Executive', 'West Country Pullman' and 'Night Riviera'; also ex South West to North East/North West/Scotland including the 'Armada', 'Devonian', 'Cornishman', 'Devon Scot' and 'Cornish Scot'. Sprinters Cardiff-Portsmouth/Brighton and services to Bath, Weston, Taunton, Weymouth and Severn Beach. South Wales main line and Birmingham route services call at Parkway. Temple Meads — 221 trains daily in 1988; Parkway — 88. Fastest services to London 1 hour 18 minutes (91.1 mph) and 1 hour 11 minutes respectively, 1938 1 hour 45 minutes (67.7 mph).

Platforms: 12, including two bays.
Facilities: ticket office, Travel Centre, refreshments, bookstall, parcels, left luggage, parking, car hire, taxis, buses.
Of special interest: station buildings, two station plaques, Bath Road depot, Severn Beach branch.

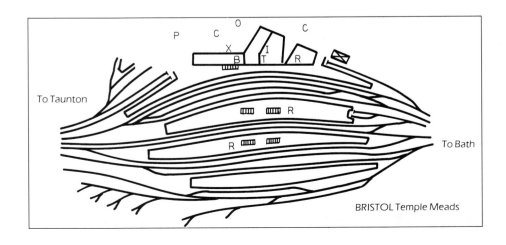

The Temple Meads approaches with the B&E building on the right and the original 1840 station on the left.

The Great Western Railway was born in Bristol and the boardroom used by the 'Bristol Committee' still looks out from the buildings of the original Brunel terminus, from which the first train departed at 8 am on 31 August 1840. Over the next five years the GWR line to London was completed, its influence was extended westwards by the Bristol & Exeter Railway, and the Midland snatched the Bristol & Gloucester company from right under its nose. The B&E opened its own station in the Temple Meads complex, linked with the GWR by a connecting curve, and that company added some handsome Jacobean-style offices opposite the 1840 terminal in 1854.

Traffic at Bristol steadily outgrew capacity and a new GWR/MR station was brought into use on 1 January 1878, owing its Gothic architectural styling to Sir Matthew Digby Wyatt. In 1935-36 the station was lengthened over the adjoining waterways and given an extra platform and two islands. It remains very much in this form, although the outer island is not now used and the trackwork was simplified in a 1970 resignalling scheme.

Although the 1840 station became non-operational in 1966, it is now being cared for by the Brunel Engineering Centre Trust, its period buildings gracefully restored and the mock hammer-beam roof preserved. With the 1854 B&E building and the dramatic frontage of the 1878 station it makes the Temple Meads approach one of the most impressive to be found anywhere. It contrasts markedly with the simple, modern station at Bristol Parkway whose two platforms and huge car park have competed very successfully with the adjacent M4 motorway since 1972.

Beneath the frontal awning at Temple Meads is a plaque to Emma Saunders, a lady whose concern earned her the title 'the railwayman's friend'. An ornate entrance area then leads to the most-used platform, No 3, where the main facilities are concentrated. Severn Beach trains are dealt with at No 1, near the panel box, and parcels traffic at the country-end bays. The great 1878 roof, recently repaired and renovated then covers four tracks and platforms 5/6, with the 1935-36 extensions beyond. Bath Road diesel depot stands at the country end of the complex.

A view of Bristol Temple Meads from Bath Road Bridge, near the diesel depot.

CAMBRIDGE

Origins: opened 1845, Eastern Counties Railway, architect Francis Thompson; rebuilt 1850, 1863 and 1908. Refurbished by BR 1987.

Location: on former GER main line to Kings Lynn, junction with lines to Hitchin and Ipswich. 55¼ miles from Liverpool Street.

Main routes: Liverpool Street-Cambridge/Kings Lynn, Cambridge-King's Cross, Cambridge-Birmingham and Cambridge-Ipswich.

Other routes: Cambridge-Norwich.

Services: main line service from Liverpool Street and on to Kings Lynn, including the 'Fenman'. Sprinters to Birmingham via Peterborough, including one Blackpool service. Electric trains on both routes to London, plus local services to Ipswich via Newmarket and Norwich via Thetford. 194 trains daily in 1988. Fastest service to London 1 hour 1 minute (54.3 mph), 1938 1 hour 5 minutes (51 mph).

Platforms: 6, including one double length and four bays.

Facilities: tickets and information, refreshments, bookstall, parcels, left luggage, parking, car hire, taxis, local buses.

Of special interest: main station

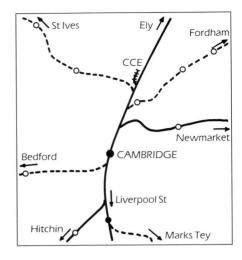

building and coats of arms, station plaques, main line working at single, long platform; also old motive power depot buildings.

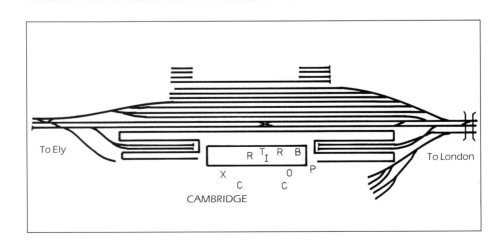

The impressive frontage at Cambridge station, designed by Francis Thompson, who also worked for the Chester & Holyhead Railway.

Long a railway centre of some importance, Cambridge station is unusual in having just one long platform for its main line services, Up trains using a midway crossover to get to the London end. Double-ended stations were commonplace in the early railway years but were steadily replaced by the standard pattern of parallel platforms, although Cambridge retained its original form and used bays to accommodate the branch line services to Bletchley, Kettering, March via St Ives, Mildenhall, Ipswich and Colchester. Cambridge used also to be served by trains to Kings Lynn and Norwich, which divided at Ely, and by the Cambridge Buffet Express services to and from King's Cross.

The Eastern Counties Railway gave Cambridge its first trains on 30 July 1845 and then defended its territory until the Great Northern finally achieved tenuous access in 1851. The Bedford & Cambridge Railway arrived 11 years later and was accommodated at the ECR station then being rebuilt. The present main platform dates from 1863 but was lengthened to 1,515 ft in 1908 and to 1,650 ft some 30 years later. In 1971 the old wooden booking offices were replaced by a modern Travel Centre and a further round of improvements, in conjunction with the Railway Heritage Trust and Cambridge City Council, was completed on 23 March 1987.

Some old locomotive depot buildings still exist beside Cambridge station but they do not spoil Francis Thompson's dramatically long colonnaded frontage, glazed now but still imposing. The newly-painted spandrels display arms of the colleges and prominent Cambridge people, and the centre arches provide access to the ticket and information office and thence to the platforms. Southbound services are electrified and those from the north end include Sprinter links to Birmingham and the North West as well as the main line to Kings Lynn and more local workings to Norwich via Ely and on the Bury St Edmunds and Ipswich line.

The traction maintenance depot north of the station maintains a tradition which once used to provide a gleaming 'B17' 4-6-0 for the royal trains to Sandringham. There is also a new panel box at the south end of the station.

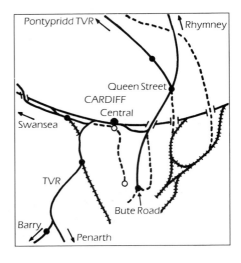

Origins: Central rebuilt 1932 on 1850 site, Great Western Railway. Queen Street 1928, station remodelled by BR.

Location: Central — South Wales main line, junction with 'Valleys' lines (on which Queen Street stands). 145¼ miles from Paddington.

Main routes: Central — South Wales main line, North West via Hereford, North East via Birmingham, and Southampton/Portsmouth.

Other routes: 'Valleys' network, Cardiff-Chepstow.

Services: Central — InterCity services West Wales-Paddington, including 'St David Executive', 'Red Dragon Pullman' and 'Hibernian', and to York/Newcastle. Sprinters to Southampton/Portsmouth and North West/North Wales. 'Valleys' trains (Central, Queen Street and Bute Road) — Barry, Penarth, Rhymney, Coryton, Merthyr Tydfil, Treherbert, and Aberdare, routes. Daily trains in 1988 — Central 494, Queen Street 306, Bute Road 54. Fastest service to London 1 hour 33 minutes (93.7 mph), 1938 2 hours 45 minutes (52.8 mph).

Platforms: Central — 6, Queen Street — 3.

Facilities: Central — ticket office, Travel Centre, refreshments, bookstalls, parcels, left luggage, car hire, taxis, bus station adjoining. Queen Street — tickets, refreshments, parking, local buses.

Of special interest: traffic working, Bute Dock museum, GWR goods depot, Barry route.

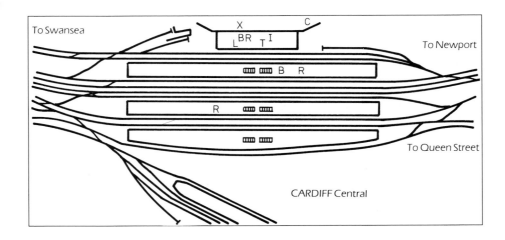

Although its facilities have been modernized, Cardiff Central still clearly displays its Great Western Railway origins.

Cardiff Central, the GWR's Cardiff General, lies on the main line through South Wales, near the heart of its capital city. The location dates from 1850 when the South Wales Railway extended the GWR route from London down the Severn and along the Bristol Channel to Swansea. By that time the Taff Vale Railway already had a docks area station at Bute Road where there is still a small terminal reached by a single line from Queen Street, Cardiff's third station and on a site previously used by the TV and Rhymney railways.

In addition to WR main line services, Cardiff Central also deals with the local trains of the 'Valleys' routes. These originated as independent lines bringing coal down to Cardiff for shipment, but now carry substantial numbers of commuters and shoppers. South of Cardiff the lines serve Barry and Penarth, traditional pleasure resorts, and to the north run to Merthyr Tydfil, Treherbert, Coryton, Aberdare and Rhymney. The 'Valleys' trains call at both Queen Street and Central on their north-south journeys.

Cardiff General was reconstructed under the 1929 Development Act using grey granite and Carrara glazed blocks. It was given a layout of two main islands and a Taff Vale island (now used by 'Valleys' trains), with another island — no longer used — for trains on the Riverside branch. The 1932 complex survives largely unaltered, the platforms reached by a tiled subway that still has the 'pointing hand' directions popular in that period. The main station buildings, which have 'wings' on either side, are lettered 'Great Western Railway' and topped by a clock tower. Inside, the facilities are located around the 186 ft main hall.

The routes from the south pass Canton maintenance depot, curve into TV platforms 5 and 6 at Central station and then, while the main line continues past the old goods depot and Pengam Freightliner terminal, curve above and over it. They meet the single line from Bute Road and then descend to Queen Street, following which the Rhymney line separates from the TVR route. A new 1928 station at Queen Street replaced the ex-RR Parade and was rebuilt in the 1970s with an island platform and a bay facility at the former Up platform.

CARLISLE CITADEL

Origins: opened 1847, Lancaster & Carlisle and Caledonian Railways, architect Sir William Tite; enlarged 1880-81.

Location: West Coast Main Line, junction with Newcastle and Whitehaven lines. 299 miles from Euston.

Main routes: West Coast Main Line plus Manchester and South/South West via Birmingham. Carlisle-Newcastle and Carlisle-Glasgow via Dumfries.

Other routes: Carlisle-Whitehaven/Barrow.

Services: InterCity services on the WCML, Euston—Scotland, including the 'Nightrider' and 'Night Caledonian' sleepers, Motorail services and the 'Clansman' and 'Royal Scot'. Manchester-Edinburgh/Glasgow, Euston-Stranraer and South/South West-Scotland services including the 'Wessex', 'Cornish' and 'Sussex' 'Scots'. Trains to Newcastle, Glasgow via Dumfries and to Whitehaven/ Barrow. 116 trains daily in 1988. Fastest service to London 3 hours 42 minutes (80.8 mph), 1938 4 hours 43 minutes (71.6 mph).

Platforms: 8, including 5 bays.

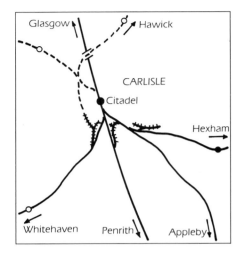

Facilities: tickets and information, refreshments, bookstall, parcels, left luggage, Motorail, car park, taxis, local buses.

Of special interest: station frontage including L&C and CR coats of arms, drinking fountains, oriel window of former signal box.

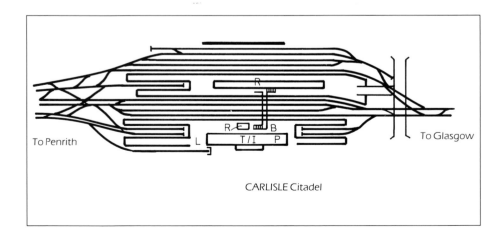

CARLISLE Citadel

Neither the rain nor the temporary ticket office can obscure the elegance of the Carlisle station frontage.

Carlisle's first railway dates from 19 July 1836 when the Newcastle & Carlisle company's line was opened as far as Blenkinsop Colliery. Opened throughout in 1838, this pioneer east-west route initially used a London Road terminus at Carlisle and shared it with the Maryport & Carlisle trains opening in 1843. Three years later the Lancaster & Carlisle and Caledonian companies obtained powers to build a station for the emerging West Coast Main Line and, after some difficulties with the Maryport & Carlisle, opened Citadel station on a former M&C site on 1 September 1847.

The new Citadel station began to be used by more and more companies. The Glasgow & South Western and Maryport & Carlisle companies joined from 1851, North British trains arrived from Hawick in 1862, the North Eastern used it from 1863 and then the services on the Midland's new Settle & Carlisle main line from 1 May 1876. All this extra traffic persuaded the Citadel Station Committee to undertake a £380,000 scheme of route remodelling and station enlargement which was brought into use on 4 July 1880. This added an island to the earlier main platform and provided a great glazed roof in harmony with the Gothic style of the original frontage which had been designed by Sir William Tite to match the city walls and the Citadel law courts. Platforms for the Furness Railway were added in 1881.

There have been other alterations over the years, like the 1973 power signal box and the 1988 new ticket and information office, but the station still retains its traditional form. The main entrance is on the Up side where the elegant two-storey frontage is topped by dormers and a central tower and fronted by an arched arcade bearing several coats of arms. An elliptical footbridge spans four running lines to platforms 1 to 3, where the other main building helps to support the ridge and furrow roof and its ironwork roundels. Platform 1 accommodates a Down platform loop with four lines in the space to the former retaining wall. The Up platform has four bays and the Down two, each with its own canopy and used by various local services. A Motorail siding stands behind the Up side bays.

CHESTER GENERAL GWR&LNWR/GWR&LMS/LMR

Origins: opened 1848, Shrewsbury & Chester Railway and Shrewsbury & Holyhead Railway, architect Francis Thompson.

Location: junction of Euston-Holyhead line with former 'North and West' route to Birkenhead and routes to Manchester via Runcorn and Northwich. 179¼ miles from Euston.

Main routes: Euston-Crewe-Chester-Holyhead and North Wales-Chester-Hull.

Other routes: Wolverhampton/Shrewsbury-Chester, Chester-Hooton, and Chester-Manchester.

Services: InterCity trains to Euston, including the 'Welsh Dragon', 'Chester Pullman' and 'Irish Mail'. North Wales/Chester cross-Pennine services to Hull via Manchester and Leeds, also to Shrewsbury with some trains extended to Wolverhampton/Birmingham/Cardiff. Services to Manchester (two routes) and to Hooton for Wirral electric interchange. 217 trains daily in 1988. Fastest service to London 2 hours 40 minutes (67.1 mph), 1938 3 hours 10 minutes (56.5 mph).

Platforms: 7, including 4 bays.

Facilities: ticket and information offices, refreshments, bookstall, parcels, left luggage, parking, car hire, taxis, local bus services.

Of special interest: station frontage, Queen's Hotel and former goods yard.

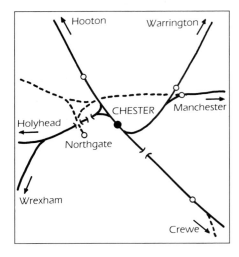

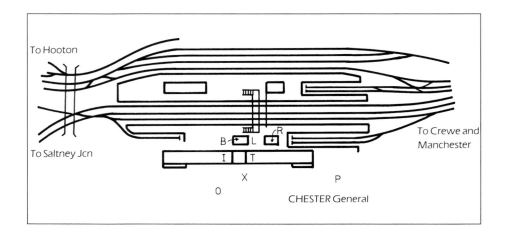

CHESTER General

The frontage of the 1848 station designed for Chester by Francis Thompson when the rail route to Holyhead was established.

Its location as a gateway to the North Wales coast and the southern approach to the Mersey made sure that Chester would attract a number of early railway schemes. Six of the seven resultant lines survive, giving the former Chester General station two routes from Manchester and one from Crewe, a Wirral line departing from the triangle at the east end of the station, and the routes to Shrewsbury and Holyhead which divide at Saltney Junction. A second station, at Chester Northgate, was used by Cheshire Lines Committee trains from Manchester Central, but this was closed on 6 October 1969.

The present station at Chester opened on 1 August 1848. Chester & Birkenhead Railway trains had been serving the city since 23 September 1840, those of the Chester & Crewe from October 1840 and of the Shrewsbury & Chester from November 1846, but 1848 was the year in which the Holyhead railway route was established, warranting a fine new joint station which the Warrington trains also used from 1850. This was a period of GWR versus LNWR infighting, eventually re-solved by traffic agreements which gave the former access to Birkenhead.

In a city known for its historic buildings, the station at the end of City Road does not let Chester down. Its 1,050 ft stone frontage was designed by Francis Thompson and consists of a two-storey facade with projecting sections, the latter with turrets in the Italian style and the whole with elaborate 'Venetian' windows. An entrance canopy with decorative ironwork leads to the main platform, while on the opposite side of Station Road the impressive Queens Hotel is linked to the station block by a passageway in the same overall style.

The original station had a single wide platform with bays at either end for local services, a single line for through trains and a transfer line beyond. More through services led to the addition of an outer island platform around 1890, provided with a separate canopy and reached by a double bridge with balustraded stairs. The freight/through lines lie beyond, with the area's servicing and engineering activity concentrated around the east-end triangle.

CLAPHAM JUNCTION LB&SCR & LSWR/SR/SR

Origins: 1904-07 reconstruction of earlier stations, London, Brighton & South Coast Railway and London & South Western Railway.

Location: intersection of ex-LSWR main and Windsor lines with former LB&SCR main line and route via Kensington Olympia. 2¾ miles from Victoria and 4 from Waterloo.

Main routes: as Waterloo (see separate entry), plus main Brighton line and Victoria-Hastings; also Brighton-Manchester/Edinburgh.

Other routes: as Waterloo plus Victoria-East Grinstead and South London lines. Clapham Junction to Kensington Olympia, Dorking and Leatherhead.

Services: as Waterloo, plus trains from Victoria on South London routes, main line to Brighton and Portsmouth, Hastings and East Grinstead lines. Brighton-Manchester/Edinburgh trains and own services to Kensington Olympia, Dorking and Leatherhead. 1,896 trains daily.

Platforms: 16 in use.

Facilities: ticket office, Travel Centre, refreshments, taxis, local buses.

Of special interest: size and intensive train working, LSWR signal post and finial on platforms 5/6, period footbridge.

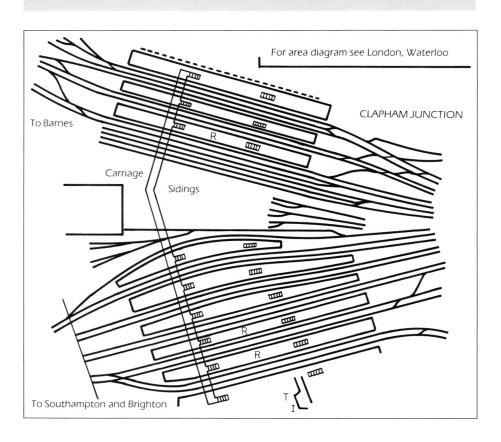

For area diagram see London, Waterloo

CLAPHAM JUNCTION

To Barnes

Carriage Sidings

To Southampton and Brighton

Clapham Junction looking towards the London termini, with a train in platform 6.

The signs at Clapham Junction proclaim it 'Britain's busiest railway station', a status justified by the hundred trains an hour which call at peak periods. Clapham Junction's importance derives from its location as the meeting point of the routes of the former London, Brighton & South Coast Railway and those of the London & South Western Railway, just before they reach their London termini. It also lies on a north-south exchange route via Kensington Olympia and has its own large volume of originating and terminating traffic.

The first station in the area was the 1838 location of the London & Southampton Railway. Twenty years later the LB&SCR line arrived, followed by the Great Western Railway, in the guise of the West London Extension Railway, in 1863. Originally, Wandsworth station, it had become Clapham Common in 1846 and then Clapham Junction in 1863, reflecting the connections between the three major railways which existed from that date. There was extensive reconstruction in 1904-07 and more recent works have created new entrance facilities within a shopping complex, but Clapham Junction remains a pretty functional place.

To accommodate its constant and complex pattern of train movements, Clapham Junction has 17 platforms (16 in use), numbering from the Up side and the longest measuring 721 ft. They cover 11.2 hectares and lie in two groups with carriage sidings between them. The Windsor/Thames Valley group consists of three islands (platforms 2 to 6) with

wooden buildings in a pleasant classical style. The other group then embraces the ex-LSWR main line routes (platforms 7-11) and those of the Central section (12-17), the latter with traditional brick buildings. The north-south trains use platform 16.

The main entrance to Clapham Junction is from the St Johns Hill side, with a passageway through the shopping complex then leading to the Travel Centre and ticket office buildings, all in modern materials. A long subway in Network South East colours then links all platforms. At the country end of the station a further link is provided by a wide footbridge, now nicely decorated and an imposing piece of period railway.

Winter fog is just lifting from the carriage siding area between the two main groups of platforms at Clapham Junction.

CREWE

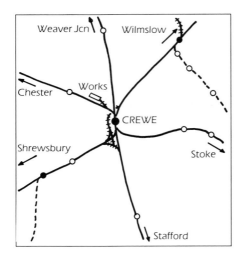

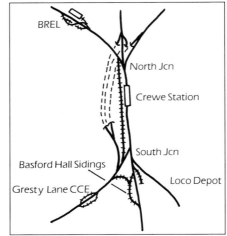

Origins: original Grand Junction station opened 1837 and grew piecemeal until rebuilt 1903-06, London & North Western Railway. Refurbished/ remodelled in 1983-85 BR scheme.

Location: West Coast Main Line, junction with Manchester, Chester, Shrewsbury and Stoke-on-Trent lines. 158 miles from Euston.

Main routes: Euston-Scotland services on West Coast Main Line; South and South West routes via Birmingham to Liverpool/Manchester and Scotland; Euston-Holyhead and Cardiff-Liverpool/Manchester.

Local routes: Derby-Crewe-North Wales, Crewe-Altrincham, Crewe-Liverpool, and Crewe-Chester-North Wales.

Services: InterCity services on West Coast Main Line from Euston/ Coventry/Birmingham to Lancaster, Blackpool and Scotland, and to Liverpool/Manchester, including the 'Merseyside Pullman', 'Manchester Pullman' and 'Lancashire Pullman', 'John Peel' and 'Clansman'. InterCity services to Holyhead, including the 'Irish Mail' and 'Welsh Dragon', and from Brighton, Poole and the South West via Bristol to Scotland, including the 'Sussex', 'Wessex', 'Devon' and 'Cornish' 'Scots'. Express Sprinter services South Wales to Manchester/ Liverpool via Shrewsbury and Crewe, Derby-Crewe-North Wales service, and local routes to Liverpool and to Altrincham, also via Chester to North Wales and Shrewsbury. 263 trains daily in 1988. Fastest service to London 1 hour 50 minutes (86.2 mph), 1938 2 hours 34 minutes (61.6 mph).

Platforms: 12, including 7 bays.

Facilities: Travel Centre and ticket office, bookstalls, refreshments, left luggage, parcels nearby, car hire, taxis, car parking nearby, local buses pass.

Of special interest: frontage contrast with period station buildings, nearby Railway Heritage Centre, area engineering and traffic activities.

The overhead wiring at Crewe has made use of the roof support columns remaining from the LNWR era.

Crewe is the outstanding example of a town which owes its existence entirely to the railway era. Until the advent of the Grand Junction Railway the only settlement in the area was the modest agricultural village of Monks Coppenhall, but this lay where the new railway crossed the Nantwich-Sandbach turnpike road, and at 8.45 am on 4 July 1837 the first train arrived at the modest platform of the infant Crewe to pick up passengers who had come in by coach or on horseback. A few days earlier, Acts authorized to the Chester & Crewe and Manchester & Birmingham Railways had started the process that would make Crewe into a junction that was later to be immortalized in song.

The line from Crewe to Chester was opened on 1 October 1840 and that to Sandbach on 10 August 1842. By this time,

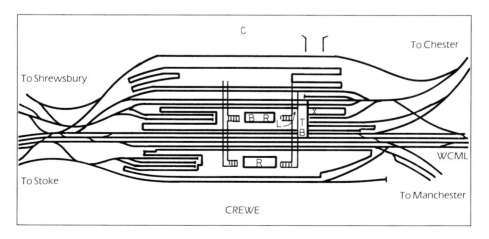

Although still a traditional station, Crewe has been given a modern frontage which houses its Travel Centre.

the Grand Junction had taken the decision to move its engineering works from Edge Hill to a more strategic location, and workshops and workers' houses were under construction around Crewe in readiness for a transfer at the beginning of 1843. In the March of that year the embryo Crewe Works came into being and two years later turned out GJR locomotive No 49, the 2-2-2 *Columbine*. From these modest beginnings was to spring a railway town, where the company provided a vast range of communal services — water, gas, education, law and order, a hospital and so on. The workshops and their community were, especially under the guidance of Francis Webb, to give the London & North Western Railway a succession of notable and capable locomotive designs.

Crewe's population rose to over 30,000 by the turn of the century, by which time its station had also changed out of all recognition. Further alterations were then made between 1903 and 1906 when an island platform was added and tunnel lines provided to allow freight trains to avoid the station area. By the middle of the century Crewe had doubled its population to 60,000 with no fewer than 10,000 of these

employed by British Rail in the various workshops, marshalling, stabling and maintenance areas, or at the station itself. Over 100,000 people weekly were journeying to and from Crewe or changing trains there.

Another round of changes came to Crewe with electrification in the 1960s. In the first year of the decade electric trains began running to Manchester, with Liverpool-Crewe services following two years later and electrification throughout to Euston by 1966. The overhead wires changed the appearance of Crewe station which also received a new frontage and forecourt. Then, in 1983, BR announced a £14.3 million scheme of resignalling and track remodelling for Crewe, to be implemented in two phases and over two years. In a series of vast, military-style operations, Crewe's old track, wiring, signalling and telecommunications were torn out and replaced by the most modern of railway equipment and a much simpler route layout. Station changes included platform lengthening, new waiting and refreshment facilities, better information systems, and new signs, ramps and lifts.

The 1983-85 changes at Crewe placed

The late running 10.28 to Blackpool runs into platform 5 at Crewe behind 90 003 on 21 October 1988.

its signalling in the hands of a new signalling control centre at North Junction, releasing the former 1938 LMS box for incorporation in the Crewe Railway Heritage Centre which houses a range of appropriate museum exhibits up to full locomotive examples.

South of the union of the Manchester, Liverpool and Chester lines, Crewe station is crossed by an overbridge which accommodates the ticketing and bookstall facilities around a small concourse. A glazed canopy extends over the vehicle access area and a footbridge leads to the stairs for the island platforms. There are three of these, although traffic is normally concentrated on the centre and Up side islands and their six bay lines.

The platforms at Crewe have been attractively painted and are linked by a second footbridge at the London end. Their modern finish is superimposed on more traditional buildings in red brick, pleasantly enlivened by bay windows and classical figureheads in stone. The earlier layout is still apparent and the partially glazed roof and its iron supports give a hint of the flavour of the station in LNWR days.

DARLINGTON BANK TOP

Origins: opened 1887, North Eastern Railway, architect William Bell. **Location:** East Coast Main Line, junction with Bishop Auckland-Saltburn line. 232½ miles from King's Cross. **Main routes:** East Coast Main Line, Newcastle-Liverpool and North East/South West route. **Other routes:** Bishop Auckland/Darlington-Saltburn and Darlington to Hartlepool, and to Whitby. **Services:** InterCity services north and south on the ECML, including the 'Talisman', 'Aberdonian', 'Tees-Tyne Pullman' and 'Cleveland Executive'. NE/SW services, Newcastle to the South West/Poole including the 'Devonian', 'Cornishman' and 'Northumbrian'. Newcastle-Darlington-Leeds-Manchester-Liverpool. Local trains to Bishop Auckland, Saltburn, Hartlepool and Whitby. 165 trains daily in 1988. Fastest service to London 2 hours 31 minutes (92.4 mph), 1938 3 hours 18 minutes (70.5 mph). **Platforms:** 4, including 2 bays. **Facilities:** Travel Centre, refreshments, bookstall, parcels, left luggage, car hire, parking, taxis, local buses pass. **Of special interest:** S&D display panels, subway mural by Brian Lee, 1886 bell from tower now mounted on platform. North Road station museum.

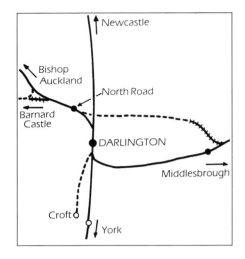

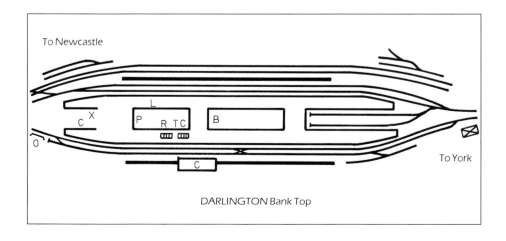

DARLINGTON Bank Top

The Down side entrance at Darlington. The bell from the tower is now mounted on the platform.

Although its once famous locomotive works have long closed, Darlington remains an important railway centre, proud of a heritage that stretches back to the opening of the Stockton & Darlington Railway in 1825. It has two stations, one dating back to S&D days and one on the East Coast Main Line, which started life in this area as the Croft branch of the pioneer S&D company. The ex-S&D station is at North Road on today's branch to Bishop Auckland, while the main line station (formerly Bank Top) is a junction between the East Coast route to Scotland and the east-west Saltburn-Bishop Auckland line.

The original route of the S&D approached Darlington via what is now the Bishop Auckland branch and crossed the later main line on the level just north of Bank Top. The surviving North Road station, with its long Georgian buildings, dates from 1842. It is now a museum, housing North Eastern Railway and S&D exhibits, with BR trains using a separate platform. The point where the two routes used to cross is marked by a signboard, and there are S&D historical display panels on the main line station.

The Great North of England Railway reached Darlington from the south in 1841 with the first section of the link on to Newcastle following four years later. The present station, however, dates from 1887 and was built when the local layout was remodelled to divert west-east trains through Bank Top instead of operating a shuttle service between the two stations. It was designed by William Bell, the NER architect at that time.

Approaching Darlington from the south, the site of Croft Yard is on the left and Geneva permanent way depot on the right. Beyond Bank Top station the 1960s diesel depot on the Down side is now out

of use and the former Bank Top steam shed opposite is no longer discernible. North Road Works has been replaced by a supermarket, but the clock there has survived.

Darlington's main line station is basically a huge island under a three-span roof linked to the main administrative buildings in the centre and supported by outer screen walls. The through lines pass around the east side of the main station which has bays at the London end and a crossover to allow separate use of each end of platform 4. There is road access from the north end overbridge but the main Down side frontage, via arches on either side of a tall clock tower and leading to a large portico, is in Park Lane. A subway then leads to the Travel Centre and other facilities grouped where it emerges on the platform.

DERBY

Origins: built 1839-41 for Midland Counties, Birmingham & Derby Junction and North Midland Railways, architect Francis Thompson. Rebuilt 1872 and 1881, frontage remodelled by BR.

Location: junction between former Midland main line and NE/SW route. 128 miles from St Pancras.

Main routes: St Pancras-Derby-Sheffield and NE/SW main lines, Birmingham-Derby-Cleethorpes and Derby-Crewe/North Wales lines.

Other routes: Sinfin/Derby-Matlock and Derby-Crewe.

Services: InterCity services Sheffield-Derby-St Pancras, including the 'Master Cutler', and South West/South Wales-Leeds/York/Newcastle, including the 'Armada', 'Devonian' and 'Cornishman', also the 'Northumbrian' (Newcastle-Poole). Sprinters Birmingham-Derby-Cleethorpes and Derby to Grantham/Skegness, and Crewe/North Wales. Local Sinfin and Matlock trains. 213 trains daily in 1988. Fastest service to London 1 hour 39 minutes (77.6 mph), 1938 2 hours 15 minutes (56.9 mph).

Platforms: 6, including one bay.

Facilities: ticket office, Travel Centre, refreshments, bookstall, parcels and left luggage, parking, car hire, taxis, local and county buses.

Of special interest: MR Railway Institute and adjacent housing, coats of arms (station) and MR wyverns (Area Manager's Office), Midland Hotel, war memorials (station and Midland Road).

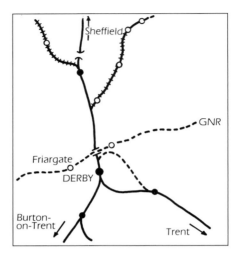

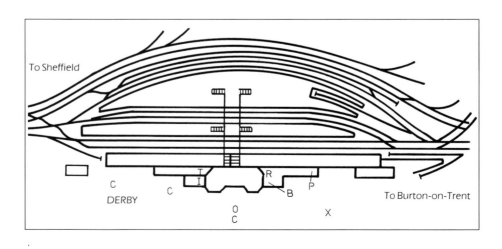

The attractive modern frontage of Derby station showing the MR and civic coats of arms.

In place of the long brick frontage of the Midland Railway station, Derby now has a new entrance area where a rising roof complements the double stairs leading to the footbridge and the two islands beyond the main Down side platform. Externally the wings on either side of the entrance carry the coats of arms of Derby and of the Midland Railway whose headquarters were here. Internally the wings house the ticket and information offices on one side and the refreshment buffet and bookstall on the other. Extensions on either side of the entrance block house parcels and administration activities.

Three pioneer railways were authorized to serve Derby in the 1836 session of Parliament, and they agreed to build a joint station on the present site. The first to open was the Midland Counties line to Nottingham, on 4 June 1839, with the Birmingham & Derby Junction route to Hampton-in-Arden following on 12 August, and then the North Midland Railway's line to Rotherham on 11 May 1840. The three companies, soon to become part of the Midland Railway, used a long station with a single main platform and end bays from that date. Extensions followed as traffic grew, including the direct London line from the south end in 1867, extra platforms in 1881 and replacement of the overall roof with the present concrete canopy supports in 1952-54.

All three of the original railways had an engine shed at Derby, that of the NMR being incorporated in the Midland's locomotive works, to which a separate

carriage and wagon works was added in the 1870s. In this century Derby Works pioneered the construction of diesel locomotives, with BR adding the Technical Centre's design and research function to the other Derby activities. The Great Northern served Derby from 1878, crossing the ornate Friargate Bridge to reach a four-platform station of the same name. It closed on 7 September 1964.

Around Derby station are clustered the 1892 Railway Institute, some MR railway housing and the Midland Hotel, said to be the world's oldest purpose-built railway hotel. On the Up side an 1839 clock tower marks the location of the former North Midland Railway locomotive roundhouse.

Opposite Derby station stands the 1892 Railway Intitute building with railway housing beyond.

DONCASTER

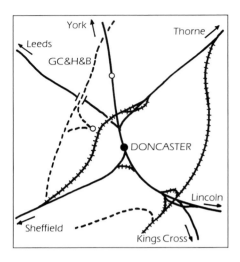

Origins: built 1849-50, Great Northern Railway; enlarged 1873-77, rebuilt 1930s.

Location: East Coast Main Line, junction with Sheffield, Wakefield, Hull, Cleethorpes and Gainsborough lines. 156 miles from King's Cross.

Main routes: King's Cross-Doncaster-Hull/Leeds/Newcastle/Scotland. Sheffield-Cleethorpes/Hull. Ex-GN&GER Joint line to Skegness/Peterborough.

Other routes: Doncaster-Selby and Scunthorpe-Doncaster-Leeds.

Services: ECML InterCity services including calls by the hourly Leeds trains, plus Hull, Newcastle and Edinburgh trains. Sprinters on the Sheffield-Humberside routes; local services to Leeds, Selby and Scunthorpe. 'Hull', 'Bradford' and 'West Yorkshire' 'Executive' trains, 'Yorkshire' and 'Hull' 'Pullmans', and the 'Talisman' all call. 235 trains daily in 1988. Fastest service to London 1 hour 40 minutes (93.4 mph), 1938 2 hours 40 minutes (58.4 mph).

Platforms: 8, including 4 bays.

Facilities: ticket office and Travel Centre, bookstall, refreshments, car hire, taxis, local buses.

Of special interest: adjacent Works, subway murals, wall drinking fountain on platform 3b.

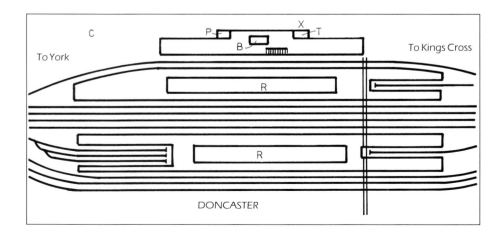

The main platforms at Doncaster with a Down HST, a cross-country Sprinter set and overhead equipment ready for electrification.

A temporary station for the Lancashire & Yorkshire trains from Knottingley was opened at Doncaster in the second half of 1848, with Great Northern services reaching the town a year later and using a site a little to the south. In 1850 the GNR gave Doncaster a permanent station in its standard, prosaic pattern, and began a London-York service in the same year. From 1852, GNR trains used the direct route via Grantham, and the South Yorkshire Railway completed the first elements of what was to become the Great Central's route from Sheffield to Doncaster and on along both banks of the Humber estuary. Later joint lines produced routes to Wakefield (GNR and MS&LR 1866) and to Gainsborough (GN&GER Joint 1867), further increasing the railway importance of Doncaster.

The East Coast Main Line route via Selby was opened in 1871 and was followed by the enlargement of Doncaster (1873-77) to give it extra outer platforms. The locomotive and carriage works also expanded considerably in the 1855-1901 period, siding accommodation was constantly being increased, and the Doncaster avoiding line was added to the complex network in 1910. A host of different railways had running powers into Doncaster and its normally busy day could reach incredible proportions on race days.

The present Doncaster station is based on a 1930s LNER rebuild and uses the Fletton bricks favoured by the company. Essentially the layout consists of two island platforms, with the main buildings and a single London-end bay on the Up side and with subway access to the Down island which has bays at each end. The BREL Works stands beyond the latter and is reached via a long footbridge over the station. The York, Humberside and West Riding routes separate north of the station, and the Sheffield and London lines to the south, where coal sidings and colliery connections surround the junction of the London and Gainsborough lines.

This traditional railway town, which produced many fine locomotives in its time, has a modern shopping complex close to the station. The subway there has murals celebrating the connection between the two, 'The Ages of the Train' and 'Welcome to Doncaster'.

The main frontage at Doncaster station, built by the LNER in a functional 1930s style.

Origins: Dover Priory opened 1861, London, Chatham & Dover Railway; Western Docks 1915, South Eastern & Chatham Railway.

Location: Priory is on the former LC&DR main line via Faversham, and Western Docks on the harbour extension thereof; Priory is 77¼ miles from Charing Cross and Victoria, Western Docks 78½ miles from the latter.

Main routes: Dover Priory to Charing Cross via Ashford, and Western Docks and Priory to Victoria via Faversham.

Other routes: Dover-Ramsgate via Deal.

Services: semi-fast electric services from Priory to Charing Cross via Ashford, and from both stations to Victoria via Faversham; also trains from Priory to Ramsgate via Deal and an all-stations service to Victoria. 40 trains daily from Western Docks in 1988, 66 from Priory. Fastest service to London 1 hour 28 minutes (52.7 mph), 1938 1 hour 40 minutes (46.3 mph).

Platforms: Priory — 3; Western Docks — 4.

Facilities: Priory — ticket office,

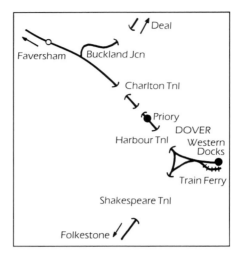

Travel Centre, refreshments, bookstall, parcels and left luggage, car hire, parking, taxis, local buses pass. Western Docks — ticket office, refreshments, bureau de change, Jetfoil terminal, buses to Hoverport terminal and Eastern Docks.

Of special interest: shipping activity and war memorial at Western Docks.

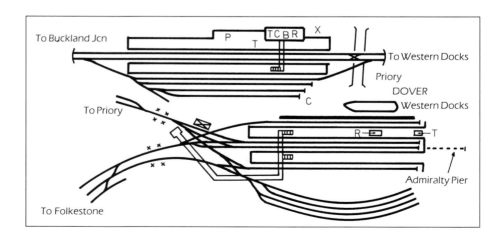

The long platforms at Dover Western Docks. The lines used to lead to the ferry terminal.

Already favoured by its proximity to the mainland of Europe, Dover grew rapidly when paddle-steamers replaced sailing vessels. Their traffic was then the lure which attracted the early railway promoters, but Parliament, over-controlling early railway schemes, decreed that the South Eastern Railway's line to Dover should take the form of a branch from Redhill on the London-Brighton line. Twenty miles longer than the route of the London-Dover road, the SER line reached a station at Dover Town on 7 February 1844.

The roundabout SER route, although subsequently shortened, was bound to suffer competition for the lucrative cross-Channel traffic. Sure enough, this duly appeared in the shape of the London, Chatham & Dover Railway's line which opened to Dover Priory, named after the former St Martin's Priory nearby, on 22 July 1861. Four months later an extension through Harbour Tunnel reached Dover Harbour station. The role of the latter has now been taken over by Dover Western Docks (formerly Dover Marine) which had begun life on 2 January 1915 handling military traffic and then converted to a civilian career on 18 January 1919.

Dover Priory is a modest, functional station located between the 158-yard Priory Tunnel and the 684-yard Harbour Tunnel. Its Down side main block is stone faced and leads to the Down platform, with an Up island over the footbridge and an Up passenger loop beyond. There are

then four mail and carriage sidings in the old goods yard area.

Dover Western Docks has all the atmosphere one would expect — long platforms beneath a multi-section lateral roof, a host of signs guiding travellers to the Calais and Ostend vessels beyond the seaward retaining wall, the Jetfoil reception on platforms 2/3, and the buses for Hoverport and Eastern Docks at the end of platforms 5/6. Quayside platforms 1 and 2 have now gone, as has the continuation of the central lines to the ferry terminal. Ferry wagons now use four sidings on the south side. Foot passengers reach the station through an ornate stone entrance and a long, elevated walkway. The ticket office is then at the seaward end, near the dramatic war memorial to former SECR and SR staff.

Dover Priory station looking towards Priory Tunnel, with a train on the Up passenger loop.

EASTBOURNE

Origins: opened 1866, London, Brighton & South Coast Railway; extended 1886.

Location: terminus of branch from Victoria-Hastings line. 66 miles from Victoria.

Main routes: Victoria-Eastbourne-Hastings and Brighton-Eastbourne-Hastings.

Other routes: Eastbourne-Haywards Heath and Eastbourne-Brighton.

Services: Victoria/London Bridge-Eastbourne-Hastings and Brighton-Eastbourne-Hastings electrics plus some London, Brighton and Haywards Heath originating and terminating services. 92 trains daily in 1988. Fastest service to London 1 hour 22 minutes (48.3 mph), 1938 1 hour 25 minutes (46.6 mph).

Platforms: 3.

Facilities: ticket office, Travel Centre, refreshments, bookstall, parcels and left luggage, parking, taxis, local buses.

Of special interest: station building architecture.

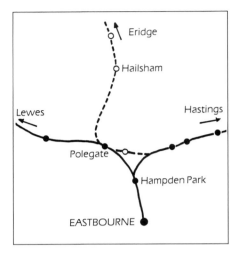

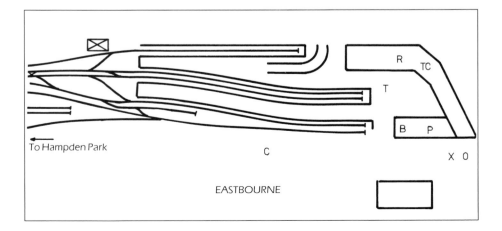

Eastbourne station proudly displaying an architectural riot of dome, clock tower and glazed lantern.

This pleasant East Sussex resort town enjoys good rail services on the Victoria-Hastings and Brighton-Hastings routes. Its elegant terminal station lies close to the shops and is not too far from the sea front.

Eastbourne today is a very different place from the small coastal village from which it grew. The location's first rail travellers warranted no more than the call of trains at Polegate on the 1846 Brighton, Lewes & Hastings Railway's line, but Eastbourne got a railway of its own with the opening of a branch from Polegate on 14 May 1849. A more direct route from Eridge via Hailsham was opened in 1880 but closed in 1968.

The coming of the railway stimulated the growth of Eastbourne to such an extent that the original station had to be replaced in 1866 when the present station was built on a new site to the east. The engineer was F. D. Banister but his work, too, was outstripped by the growth in traffic and the London, Brighton & South Coast Railway had to enlarge the location 20 years later. The Southern, too, had to create more accommodation but, in more

recent years, the closure of the adjoining goods depot has enabled part of the site to be given over to car parking and to a specialist shopping development in the old goods shed.

Eastbourne retains its elegant station buildings with street-side awnings covering the pavements. The main block is angled in the centre where a fine, highly-embellished clock tower occupies the corner position. The building to the right has a domed section and that to the left a raised roof section surmounted by the sort of ornamental glazed lantern of which the LB&SCR seemed rather fond. Bus, taxi and parking facilities exist to the side of the main frontage while inside a pleasant concourse is surrounded by the ticket, refreshment, bookstall and other travel support units. Three platforms are now in use, with an additional Down side line for parcels and mail.

The inland side of Eastbourne is served by the modest two-platform station at Hampden Park on the section to the triangular junction with the Brighton-Hastings line.

EDINBURGH WAVERLEY HAYMARKET

Origins: Waverley — new station built 1892-1902 on 1846 site, North British Railway; remodelled by BR 1988-89. Haymarket — opened 1842, Edinburgh & Glasgow Railway, refurbished by BR.

Location: both stations are on the East Coast Main Line, and are 393½ miles and 394¾ miles from King's Cross respectively.

Main routes: East Coast Main Line from King's Cross and on to Dundee and Aberdeen. Euston-Edinburgh-Perth/Inverness. Edinburgh-South and South West. Edinburgh-Glasgow via Falkirk.

Other routes: Edinburgh to Dunfermline/Kirkcaldy, to Stirling/Dunblane, to West Calder/Glasgow via Shotts, to Bathgate, and to North Berwick.

Services: InterCity services on East Coast Main Line to Newcastle/Leeds/King's Cross and north to Dundee/Aberdeen, including the 'Talisman', 'Flying Scotsman', 'Highland Chieftain' and 'Aberdonian'. Services via the West Coast Main Line to Euston, including sleepers and the 'Clansman', and to Brighton/Poole/Penzance via Birmingham, including sleepers and the 'Wessex Scot', 'Devon Scot', 'Sussex Scot' and 'Cornishman'. Scot-Rail expresses to Glasgow, Perth/Inverness and Dundee/Aberdeen, plus local services to Dunfermline/Kirkcaldy, to Stirling/Dunblane, to West Calder/Glasgow via Shotts, to Bathgate, and to North Berwick. Virtually all trains call at both stations to give Waverley 370 trains daily in 1988 and Haymarket 367. Fastest service from the former to London 4 hours 25 minutes (89.1 mph), 1938 6 hours (65.6 mph).

Platforms: Waverley — 12 in use; Haymarket — 4.

Facilities: Waverley — Travel Centre, refreshments, shops, bookstall, parcels, left luggage, car hire, parking, taxis, local buses pass. Haymarket — ticket office, bookstall, local buses pass.

Of special interest: ex-North British Hotel, Waverley's former booking office area and station plaques.

Construction activity has been continuing in the Edinburgh area in preparation for the completion of the electrification of the East Coast Main Line which will give the Scottish capital electric train services from May 1991. In addition to works in the station and the tunnel approaches, the Millerhill depot construction teams have now taken on the newly-approved electrification of the link from the West Coast Main Line at Carstairs.

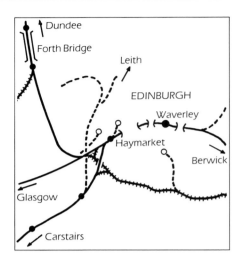

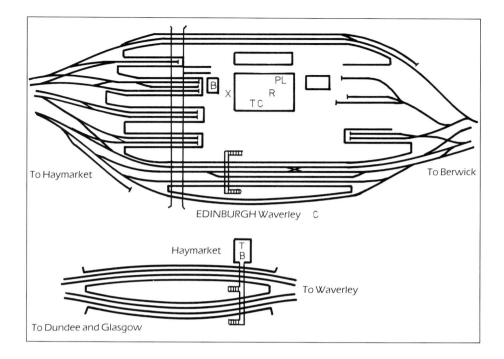

To Haymarket

To Berwick

EDINBURGH Waverley   C

Haymarket

To Waverley

To Dundee and Glasgow

Over two million visitors enjoy Edinburgh's attractions every year, many of them arriving via Waverley station which lies in the valley between the Old Town and modern Edinburgh, adjacent to Princes Street, the castle and the gardens. It is a large and extremely interesting location but is overshadowed, literally and architecturally, by the adjacent North British Hotel which was opened by the North British Railway in 1902 on a superb site in the angle between Princes Street and South Bridge.

The Caledonian Railway's Princes Street terminus closed in 1965, but Edinburgh has a second major station at Haymarket, further along the East Coast Main Line and just before the routes for Carstairs and Glasgow peel off. Beyond Haymarket, which is the station for Edinburgh Airport and has a BR maintenance depot nearby, the ECML turns north for the Firth of Forth and the dramatic 1½ mile crossing of the Forth Bridge.

Edinburgh's first railway was the horse-worked line of the Edinburgh & Dalkeith Railway which was brought into service in 1831. Passenger trains started working out of St Leonards a year later, the system

eventually being acquired and brought up to date by the North British Railway. The latter had opened its route to Berwick on 22 June 1846, using a station on the Waverley site, and it was joined there on 1 August by the Edinburgh & Glasgow Railway with an extension of the route it had opened from Glasgow to Haymarket on 21 February 1842. This two-railway origin is still apparent at Waverley in its combination of north and south end terminating lines plus through platforms on the Market Street side.

The Edinburgh & Glasgow company, soon to be in competition with the 1848 Caledonian line from Carstairs, established its administration in what is now the Haymarket station building. This is a modest two-storey rectangular block in stone, with a four-column Doric portico and central clock providing the embellishment and adding to the classical Georgian impression. From the ticket office and bookstall area a modern glazed footbridge leads to the combination of centre island and two outer platforms immediately following the Haymarket tunnels. The platforms, also modernized, have flat canopies in place of the old iron-

Edinburgh Haymarket station, in a classical Georgian style, was the headquarters of the Edinburgh & Glasgow Railway. Now it serves the airport and the Gallery of Modern Art.

framed roof which went to the Bo'ness & Kinneil Railway.

The line between Haymarket and Waverley stations is partly in tunnels, the trains emerging from those beneath The Mound to pass through Princes Street Gardens and enter either the north end terminal platforms at Waverley or one of the through ones. With the exception of the trains to North Berwick, all the services

A view of the north end of Edinburgh Waverley with Princes Street Gardens on the left and the North British Hotel beyond.

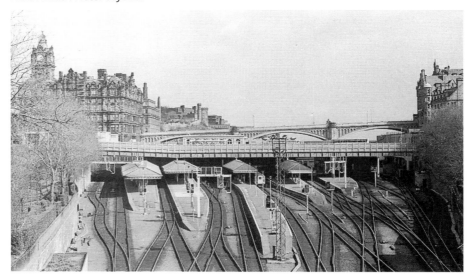

Edinburgh Waverley station looking towards the through platforms and with the ticket and administration block on the left.

originating or terminating at Waverley use the north end of the station, allowing the south end to be remodelled in 1988. The former bay platform area there has now largely been given over to functional platforms for Royal Mail, parcels and Motorail traffic. Further remodelling is to follow completion of the work at the south end.

The North Bridge road linking Market and Princes Streets crosses Waverley station and two access roads descend to platform level between the ends of the bays. The roadway linking these two also extends along the side of the through platform 10/11 to the motorail bay at the south end. Behind, and taking up most of the area between the two 'terminal' parts of the station, is the two-storey office block. Within this the former ticket hall was restyled in 1986 to provide Travel Centre, refreshment and other facilities. A link with the past survives in the elaborate, domed ceiling where garlanded cherubs cavort amid a wealth of scrolled ironwork. The outside of the building accommodates the North British Railway war memorial, a quaintly-lettered reminder that the building was used as a Forces Rest Room in the First World War, and a plaque recording the origin of the Royal Botanic Gardens from the seventeenth-century Royal Physic Garden which was located nearby.

When Waverley was rebuilt in 1892-1902, conservation and other pressures limited it to a low-profile affair, largely hidden beneath the ridge and furrow roof and with the wooden booking office the greatest extravagance. No such constraints affected the contemporary North British Hotel nearby, nor the Caledonian Hotel opened one year later, in 1903. The high, sandstone rectangle of the former is relieved by some exuberant roof embellishments with more decoration on the South Bridge frontage. The Caledonian's four-storey building has a tiered attic-end dormer and a collection of Dutch gables to offset its lower severity.

Origins: St Davids opened 1848, rebuilt 1864 and 1911-14, Great Western Railway; Central opened 1860, rebuilt 1933, London & South Western Railway.

Location: St Davids is on the GWR West of England main line, 173¼ miles from Paddington; Central is on the former LSWR main line, 171¾ miles from Waterloo.

Main routes: St Davids — West of England main line and NE/SW services to North East, North West and Scotland. Also via Central to Waterloo.

Other routes: St Davids-St Thomas-Paignton and Exmouth-Central-St Davids-Barnstaple.

Services: InterCity services from St Davids to Paddington and via Central to Waterloo, also to North East, North West and Scotland via Birmingham. Sleeper service to London and prestige trains including the 'Cornish Riviera' and 'Night Riviera', 'Brunel Executive', 'Golden Hind Pullman', 'Devon Scot' and 'Cornish Scot', 'Devonian', 'Cornishman' and 'Armada'. St Davids 152 trains daily in 1988, Central 88. Fastest service to London 1 hour 59 minutes (88.6 mph), 1938 2 hours 55

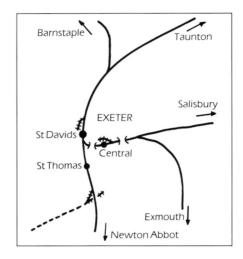

minutes (59.6 mph).

Platforms: St Davids — 7, including one bay; Central — 3.

Facilities: St Davids — ticket office, Travel Centre, refreshments, bookstall, parcels, left luggage, car park, taxis and buses; Central — tickets, information, buses and left luggage.

Of special interest: estuarial lines to Exmouth and Newton Abbot; SDR pumping station, now a museum, at Starcross.

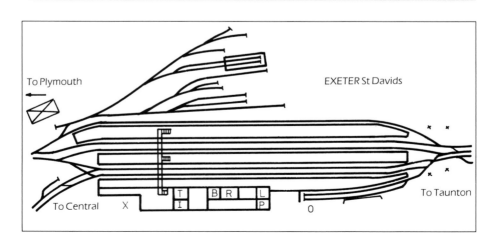

Exmouth and Barnstaple dmus at Exeter Central with the main station buildings in the background.

Exeter has three stations, the main one — St Davids — lying on the West of England main line from Paddington to Penzance. St Thomas, on the same line but served only by local trains, originated with the atmospheric South Devon Railway, while Central is the station on the former LSWR route from Waterloo.

The single-sided station, opened when the Bristol & Exeter Railway reached the latter point in 1844, was replaced in 1864 after the opening of the connecting line between the LSWR and GWR routes. By Henry Lloyd and Francis Fox, this, in turn, was overlaid by 1911-14 alterations which added a two-storey frontage and replaced the overall roof with awnings. The curious 1860 Queen Street LSWR station, with its two-storey wooden buildings with a verandah and staggered twin roof, was replaced in 1933 when the 'Central' suffix was also brought into use.

St Davids station lies just over ¼ mile west of the city centre. The long stone frontage, still displaying the GWR logo, is backed by one of the 1864 retaining walls and a glazed clerestory from the same period. Beyond the main Down platform come two islands reached by footbridge and dealing with Up main line and local trains. There are servicing sidings on the Down side, more stock and freight sidings plus the modern panel box on the Up, and a barrier crossing at the London end of the complex.

Although it no longer has an overall roof, the Italian frontage at St Thomas station is worth a visit, while Exeter Central is a good example of its 1933 period. The curved street-level building houses shops as well as the BR offices, from which a tiled footbridge leads to the long lower level platforms, the Down one with a bay and the Up side with a cement depot in the former goods yard. The area of the former centre lines has been landscaped and the station is well used, partly by passengers to and from the nearby shopping centre. The Devon County Prison building overlooks the site.

The two main stations at Exeter derive a useful connecting service from the Waterloo trains to and from St Davids and from the Exmouth-Barnstaple workings.

The local pilot passes through the Up main platform at Exeter St Davids with tank wagons from Canal Basin.

GATWICK AIRPORT

Origins: opened by BR 1958 on site of 1891 Gatwick Racecourse station. Rebuilt by BR 1967-68.
Location: ex-LB&SCR London-Brighton main line. 26¾ miles from Victoria.
Main routes: Gatwick Airport to Victoria, to Bedford (Thameslink), and to Reading via Guildford. Victoria-Gatwick-Brighton/Portsmouth.
Other routes: London Bridge/Gatwick-Brighton, and Victoria-Gatwick-Horsham/Burgess Hill.
Services: Gatwick Express trains non-stop to and from Victoria, Thameslink trains to Bedford and InterCity services Victoria to Brighton/Littlehampton/Bognor Regis/Portsmouth Harbour. Also Victoria/Gatwick-Horsham/Burgess Hill trains, slower electrics on Brighton line and dmu service via Guildford to Reading. 466 trains daily in 1988. Fastest service to London 30 minutes (53.5 mph), 1938 37 minutes (43.4 mph).
Platforms: 6.
Facilities: tickets and information, bookstall, taxis, bureau de change, further facilities in airport terminals.
Of special interest: general station complex and links with airport,

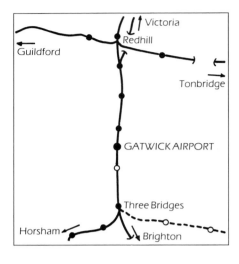

Gatwick Express push-and-pull working with Class '73' locomotives.

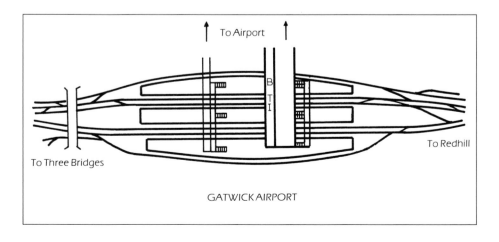

GATWICK AIRPORT

Locomotive 73 211 draws into Gatwick Airport with one of the Gatwick Express services in December 1988.

The Gatwick location started life in 1891 serving racegoers and bearing the name Gatwick Racecourse. It then began a different career when a new station was opened to serve the infant airport on 30 September 1935. Initially called Tinsley Green and provided with 63 services a day, this location took the name Gatwick Airport on 1 June the following year. The 1935 station then lasted until 1958 when it was replaced by the present one, on the site of the original Gatwick Racecourse and rebuilt into its present form in 1967-68. The Tinsley Green platforms are still visible south of its modern replacement which is now the leading BR example of the provision of special facilities for air travellers.

To cater for the millions who use the trains to commence or complete their air journeys, BR provides separate ticketing, platform and luggage facilities at Victoria, a non-stop Gatwick Express service to Gatwick Airport every 15 minutes, and a station there directly connected to the British Airports Authority terminals. The Victoria-Gatwick service operates virtually all day every day with 138 Gatwick Express trains taking just 30 minutes on the journey.

The station at Gatwick Airport consists of three island platforms with easy links to the north and south air terminals. The lines through platforms 1, 2, 3 and 6 are reversible to cater for terminating trains which include the multiple units to and from Reading and the Thameslink services to Bedford; the latter normally use platform 6. The Gatwick Express trains use numbers 1 and 2, and are worked by Class '73' locomotives which arrive with the locomotive leading and then remain that way for the return journey.

The main links between the platforms and the airport are the lifts, stairs and escalators at the London end of the station. These rise to a wide bridge area integrated with the main concourse and providing bureau de change and other facilities in addition to those covering tickets and information. Finished in the same modern materials as the platform buildings, this area has an overall roof on a tubular support structure in much the same style as the one at London Bridge.

Origins: Central — opened 1879, Caledonian Railway, architect Sir R. R. Anderson; extended 1901-05, architect James Miller. Queen Street — new station on 1842 site in 1877, North British Railway, engineer James Carswell; remodelled by BR.

Location: Central — terminus of West Coast Main Line, of ex-G&SWR routes via Kilmarnock and of Clyde Coast lines. 401¼ miles from Euston. Queen Street — terminus of Edinburgh, Perth and West Highland lines.

Main routes: Central — WCML, to Brighton/Poole/Penzance lines via Birmingham and to Manchester. Queen Street — ECML via Edinburgh, to Aberdeen/Inverness via Perth and to West Highlands.

Other routes: Central — to Gourock/Wemyss Bay, Stranraer, Ardrossan/Largs/Ayr, East Kilbride/Carlisle via Dumfries and to Edinburgh via Shotts; Low Level — Dalmuir-Motherwell/Circle/Lanark. Queen Street — to Falkirk, Stirling and Dunblane; Low Level — Balloch/Helensburgh-Airdrie.

Services: Central — InterCity services over WCML to Euston including the 'Royal Scot', 'Nightrider' and 'Night Caledonian'; on the Brighton/Poole/Penzance routes, including the 'Devon Scot', 'Wessex Scot', 'Cornish Scot' and 'Sussex Scot'; and to Manchester. Services to Stranraer for the Larne steamers, to Edinburgh via Shotts, and to Carlisle via Dumfries. Local trains to Ayrshire and Renfrewshire Coast with links to Firth of Clyde steamers. Low Level — Argyle Line electrics Dalmuir-Motherwell/Circle/Lanark. Queen Street — ScotRail InterCity trains to Edinburgh and ECML, to Perth-Aberdeen/Inverness and trains to Oban, Fort William and Mallaig, local Dumbarton and Stirling services, including Balloch/Helensburgh-Airdrie electrics from Low Level. Daily trains

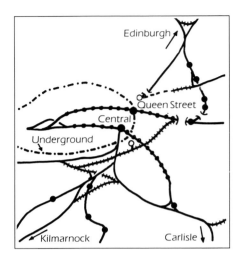

in 1988, Central 724 (plus Low Level 150) and Queen Street 195 (plus Low Level 204). Fastest service to London 5 hours 1 minute (80 mph), 1938 6 hours 30 minutes (61.7 mph).

Platforms: Central — 11 plus 2 Low Level; Queen Street — 7 plus 2 Low Level.

Facilities: Central — Travel Centre, ticket office, bookstalls, refreshments and bar, shops, parcels, left luggage, taxis, local buses pass, service to Queen Street. Queen Street — tickets and information, refreshments, shops, bookstall, parcels and left luggage, parking, taxis, local buses pass, service to Central, Buchanan Street underground nearby.

Of special interest: Central Hotel and station frontage, Caledonian war memorial and shopping centre. Museum of Transport in Burnhouse Road.

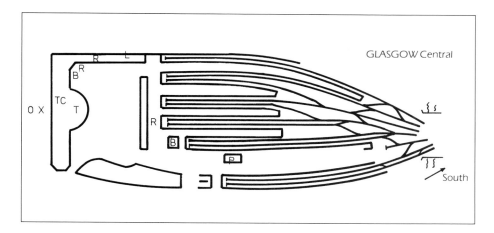

GLASGOW Central

South

Scotland's coal deposits led to early canals being supplemented by wagonways and, in turn, to an early use of railways. The Glasgow & Garnkirk Railway opened in September 1831 and was followed by Greenock, Ayr and Edinburgh schemes which were operational by 1842. By the middle of the century there were three trunk rail routes from the south, those of the Caledonian and Glasgow & South Western Railways linking Carlisle with Glasgow and the North British line completing the East Coast route from Berwick.

The Edinburgh & Glasgow Railway opened on 21 February 1842 using Queen Street station at Glasgow for its eight daily trains. Access to the station then, as now, was via a tunnel of 1 mile 33 yards built at the insistence of the Port Dundas canal owners and with a 1 in 42 gradient which needed a winding engine to start trains on

their 2½-hour journey. The North British Railway rebuilt the original Queen Street station in 1877 and acquired the North British Hotel in George Square at the same period.

Queen Street station today deals with trains on the lines to Edinburgh, Perth and the West Highlands, plus Lanark/Motherwell/Airdrie to Milgavie/Balloch/Helensburgh services via its Low Level platforms. The main station, extensively modernized by BR, lies behind George Square and has a shopping/facilities arcade running from North Hanover Street to Dundas Street across the platform end concourse. Six platforms and one bay are accommodated beneath the single span elliptical roof which is supported on substantial pillars with a top decoration of Prince of Wales' feathers. Beyond the platform ends the lines converge upon the surviving tunnel

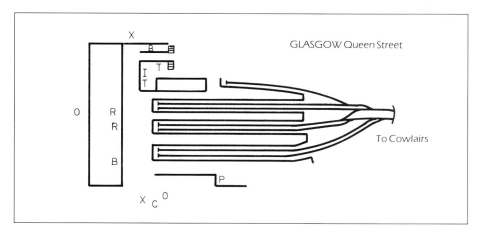

GLASGOW Queen Street

To Cowlairs

A view of the main platforms at Glasgow Central with a West Coast Main Line train standing at platform 1.

bore and its two 50 mph bi-directional tracks. A modern operations depot stands behind No 1 platform, but beyond this the stone walls of the 1877 station are still visible.

The nearby Buchanan Street terminus of the Caledonian Railway was closed on 7 November 1966 but has given its name to the underground station adjoining Queen Street. Its entrance is opposite the one to the Queen Street Low Level station which comprises two outer platforms and a central support island.

The Caledonian Railway completed its line from Carlisle on 15 February 1848. Although it had powers to cross the Clyde, the 'Caley' originally used a small terminus south of the river, known as Southside. Services on the Glasgow & South Western Railway route from Carlisle via Kilmarnock

The concourse at Glasgow Central. The Central Hotel rises above the ticket office and Travel Centre straight ahead.

used Bridge Street, and later Dunlop Street, while CR services generally ran into Buchanan Street via Coatbridge until the idea of crossing the river was revived and an Act of Parliament obtained in 1873 (revised 1875).

The new viaduct across the Clyde was completed in 1878 having cost some £64,000. It was opened the following July along with the new Central terminus which had absorbed 10 million bricks and 14,000 tons of cast iron. From 1 August 1879, the six main platforms of the new station took over from Southside and it was soon handling 300 trains a day. Traffic continued to grow, making it necessary to extend the station. This was done between 1901 and 1905, increasing the number of platforms to 13, doubling the approach lines, and allowing the number of trains to rise to 600 a day. By this time the Caledonian Railway was also operating the Low Level station, although this was to be closed in 1964 until the revival of local Glasgow services in conjunction with the Strathclyde PTE.

The Central station frontage is in Gordon Street, 650 yards from Queen Street. Seven iron pillars support the glazed *porte-cochère* arcade with the BR Travel Centre behind and the stone edifice of the Central Hotel rising above. Both station and hotel feature ornate ironwork in their entrances, but once the concourse is reached a much more modern impression prevails. This is partly due to the £1.5 million shopping facility executed in glass and dark wood-work and provided with an external lift capsule. Beyond lie the 13 platforms under two sections of ridge and furrow roofing, that on the main-line side parallel with the platforms and the section over the staggered suburban side and Low Level escalators carried on transverse supports to the outer wall with its glazed fan apertures. The Low Level station consists of a single island platform approached past period double iron columns, but sufficiently modern to have won a 1980 Business & Industry Premier Award.

Although a number of Glasgow stations have closed, like the great GSWR St Enoch which replaced Dunlop Street, railways remain alive and well in and around the city and many worthwhile buildings survive in addition to the two major operational terminals at Central and Queen Street.

A view from the platforms at Glasgow Queen Street towards the steeply graded tunnel exit from the station.

Origins: station and port opened 1883, Great Eastern Railway, H. H. Poswell.

Location: on Harwich branch from Liverpool Street-Norwich main line. 69 miles from Liverpool Street.

Main routes: Harwich-Parkeston Quay-Liverpool Street. Parkeston Quay-Blackpool/Liverpool/Manchester.

Other routes: Parkeston Quay-Liverpool Street boat trains.

Services: London-Amsterdam Euro-City services 'Admiraal de Ruyter' and 'Benjamin Britten'. Sprinter service to Blackpool/Liverpool/Manchester, including the 'Loreley'. Regular emu service Harwich-Parkeston Quay-Liverpool Street. 58 trains daily (plus boat specials) in 1988. Fastest service to London 1 hour 15 minutes (55.2 mph), 1938 1 hour 33 minutes (44.5 mph).

Platforms: 3, including one bay.

Facilities: tickets and information, refreshments, bookstall, parcels and left luggage, parking, taxis, shipping offices.

Of special interest: Harwich Society and St John's Ambulance station plaques; shipping, cranage and traffic activity. Also Harwich Town station,

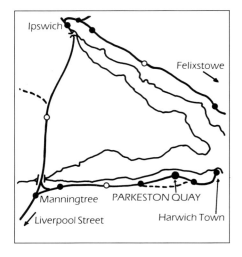

plaques, ferry terminal and former GER hotel.

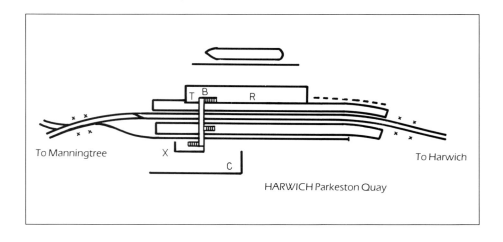

HARWICH Parkeston Quay

Harwich Parkeston Quay in 1988 with a EuroCity boat train in the Down platform and an emu from Liverpool Street in the Up.

Most of the East Anglian estuaries had ambitions to be part of a rail and ship route to Europe. Even the tiny Kelvedon & Tollesbury Light Railway joined in the competition but could hardly match the resources of the Great Eastern Railway which concentrated on the 1854 Harwich branch and began running its own steamers from Harwich proper nine years later. A hotel was added there soon after.

A desire for expansion led the Great Eastern to transfer some of its business to a new port further up the Stour estuary. This was Parkeston Quay, named after the GER chairman Charles Parkes and opened on 15 March 1883. To cater for its additional traffic, the branch was doubled as far as the main line. In the LNER years the port grew to nearly 4,000 ft of deep-water quay and handled services like the 'Antwerp', 'Flushing' and 'Hook Continentals', with the Zeebrugge train ferry operating from Harwich proper at the end of the single line section east of the Parkeston complex.

A terminal station was added at Parkeston Quay West in 1934 but closed in 1972, leaving the present Down platform to handle EuroCity boat trains. The Liver-pool Street-Harwich emus use the Up platform which is also the start of the single line on through Dovercourt Bay to Harwich Town. Next to the Parkeston Down platform stands H. H. Poswell's long two-storey terminal building, now occupied by the Sealink, DFDS and Fred Olsen shipping offices which provide facilities in connection with the shipping routes to Hook of Holland, Esjberg, Hamburg, Gothenberg, Christiansen, Cuxhaven and Hertshals, Oslo. In warm red brick with plenty of decorative stone dressing, the building is topped by a parapeted clock tower.

In 1968 BR strengthened the quay at Parkeston, provided new storage sheds and installed two mammoth container cranes. New vessels were also put into the fleet as part of the overall plan to move from the old wagon-load age into the new one of containerized and roll-on roll-off freight movement. These changes have also affected the port back-up areas where the remaining freight sidings are now used for block train loads of cars and similar traffics of the modern age.

HEREFORD BARR'S COURT

Origins: built 1854-56, Shrewsbury & Hereford Railway, R. E. Johnston.
Location: Newport-Shrewsbury line, junction with Worcester/Oxford line. 149¾ miles from Paddington.
Main routes: Cardiff-Newport-Hereford-Shrewsbury/Crewe and Hereford-Worcester-Oxford/Paddington.
Local routes: Hereford-Worcester/Birmingham.
Services: InterCity 125 services to Paddington, including the 'Cathedrals Express' and 'Cotswold Express'. Sprinters on Cardiff-Newport-Hereford-Shrewsbury-Crewe/Liverpool/Manchester services, and to Oxford. Local services to Birmingham New Street via Worcester. 70 trains daily in 1988. Fastest service to London 2 hours 36 minutes (57.6 mph), 1938 3 hours 25 minutes (43.8 mph).
Platforms: 4, including one bay.
Facilities: tickets and information, refreshments and small bookstall, parcels and left luggage, parking, taxis, local buses nearby.
Of special interest: Bulmer Railway Centre, GWR roundel platform seats, Malvern line (tunnels and Great Malvern station).

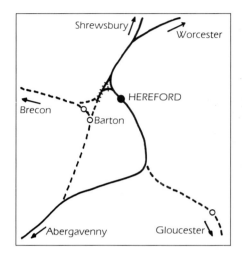

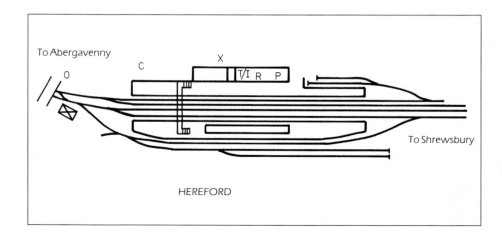

HEREFORD

A view of Hereford station looking south, with the main Down side platform and buildings on the right.

At one time or another Hereford has had five radiating railway lines and three main stations, reflecting its importance as a railhead and it strategic significance to the early railways seeking to penetrate mid-Wales or to tap the lucrative South Wales coal traffic. Although the city's rail routes have now been reduced to three, all of which use one remaining station just east of the main shopping area, Hereford continues to represent a major rail facility for a large and pleasant area of Anglo-Welsh border country.

Goods train traffic began on the Shrewsbury & Hereford Railway's line from Ludlow in mid-1852, with a through passenger service from Shrewsbury commencing on 6 December the following year. The S&H trains used the present station site, then occupied by a private house which gave its Barr's Court name to the station complex which was developed to accommodate additional traffic from the Newport, Abergavenny & Hereford Railway's line to the south (1854) and the Great Western Railway route from Gloucester (1855). The Worcester route, for many years to carry the GWR expresses to Paddington, was completed in 1861, with the Midland Railway's line west to Three Cocks Junction being added to the Hereford network eight years later. Early stations at Barton (GWR) and Moorfields (MR) relinquished their passenger services to the GWR & LNWR joint location at Barr's Court, but continued as goods depots.

Hereford station comprises a main Down side platform with a period foot-bridge leading to the Up island. The tall and narrow two-storey main block in red brick has decorative end gables and nine tall chimneys along the steeply pitched roof. In contrast, the island buildings are much simpler and the north end goods shed is austerely functional. There is some good ironwork on the station and a traditional signal box at the south end.

The Bulmer Railway Centre in Whitecross Road, Hereford, is the home of GWR No 6000 *King George V*, LMS No 6201 *Princess Elizabeth* and SR No 35028 *Clan Line*. There are static displays at weekends from April to September, plus special steaming days.

The long narrow station building at Hereford with its tall chimneys and gables and steeply pitched roof.

HOLYHEAD

Origins: 1880 London & North Western Railway station remodelled by BR 1988-89.

Location: Isle of Anglesey terminus of route from London, and port for shipping services to and from Ireland (Dun Laoghaire). 263½ miles from Euston.

Main routes: Euston-Crewe-Holyhead and Holyhead-Hull.

Other routes: Holyhead-Llandudno and Holyhead-Chester-Crewe.

Services: InterCity services to Euston, including the 'Irish Mail', also special boat trains. Sprinters to Hull via Manchester and some Chester line services extended to Derby, Cardiff etc. Local trains to Llandudno. 34 trains daily in 1988. Fastest service to London 4 hours 32 minutes (58.2 mph), 1938 5 hours 10 minutes (51 mph).

Platforms: 3.

Facilities: tickets and information, refreshments, parcels and left luggage, parking, taxis, local buses pass.

Of special interest: shipping berths and activity, container terminal; also former lairage area for handling the Irish cattle business.

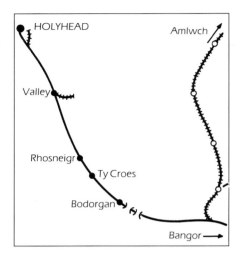

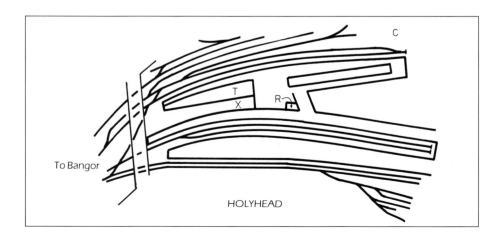

The Up side at Holyhead with the container terminal on the right. Work was beginning on a remodelling scheme at the time of this picture.

Holyhead is the British port for the principal surface route to Dublin. It lies on the northern coast of the Holy Island peninsula in the extreme west of the Isle of Anglesey and can trace its history as the major port for Ireland back to the years of the first Queen Elizabeth. The era of Holyhead's main growth began in 1810 when John Rennie began building a new harbour. Thomas Telford was engaged to improve the road access route and in 1826 his notable bridge across the Menai Strait replaced the troublesome ferry crossing of earlier times.

Although the Irish mails were routed via Liverpool once that city got a rail link to London, Holyhead was restored to pre-eminence with the arrival of the Chester & Holyhead Railway which opened to a temporary station at the port on 1 August 1848, the Britannia Bridge coming into use two years later to complete the scenic route from Chester along the North Wales coast. The Great Breakwater was added in 1870 and ten years later a new station, with a hotel, replaced the 1851 location at the south end of the inner harbour.

Holyhead suffered a setback when the Britannia Bridge was destroyed by fire in 1970, but this has been rebuilt and trains restored to the 22-mile stretch of line across Anglesey's pastoral landscape. Nearing Holyhead station there are the remains of a large lairage area, a reminder of the former shipments of cattle from Ireland which were then conveyed away by the train-load for fattening prior to slaughter. The terminal then follows the access road overbridge, with the hotel site in the centre and platforms each side of the berthing basin. On the Down side are the train servicing sidings and carriage washing plant and on the Up a container terminal.

Like most such locations Holyhead (Caergybi) comes to life before the departure or after the arrival of the shipping services. These are provided by Sealink sailings to and from Dun Laoghaire and those of B&I to Dublin Ferryport. The station has a modern passenger-handling building alongside platform No 1 and work began in 1988 on a scheme of remodelling the period red brick buildings of the 1880 station.

HUDDERSFIELD

Origins: built 1847-50 for the Huddersfield & Manchester Railway & Canal Company, architect J. P. Pritchett.

Location: on the Manchester-Leeds cross-Pennine main line, junction with Barnsley/Sheffield line. 25½ miles from Manchester.

Main routes: cross-Pennine routes North Wales-Hull, Liverpool-Scarborough and Liverpool-Newcastle.

Other routes: Manchester/Marsden-Leeds, Huddersfield-Leeds and Huddersfield-Wakefield.

Services: InterCity services Liverpool-Newcastle and cross-Pennine Sprinters North Wales-Hull and Manchester-York/Scarborough. Local trains to Manchester, Leeds and Wakefield. 138 trains daily in 1988. Fastest service to Manchester 37 minutes (41.3 mph), 1938 40 minutes (38.1 mph).

Platforms: 5, including 2 bays.

Facilities: tickets and information, bookstall, buffet, parcels, left luggage, car park, taxis, local buses.

Of special interest: main station building, goods yard buildings, H&M and LYR coats of arms, ticket office mural, scenic routes to Manchester and Barnsley.

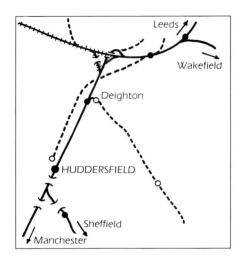

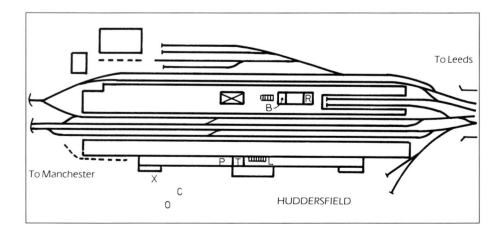

A Sprinter unit stands in the north-end bay at Huddersfield. Note the goods warehouse building on the right.

The imposing station backing St George's Square at Huddersfield carries the coats of arms of two railway companies, the Huddersfield & Manchester Railway & Canal Co and the Lancashire & Yorkshire Railway. The former represented a combination of railway and canal interests and beat off several rival schemes to open a line north from Huddersfield on 3 August 1847 and south to Stalybridge on 1 August two years later. Despite capitalizing on the experience of its canal predecessor, the valley situation of Huddersfield caused the H&M a great many construction problems to which the tunnels and viaducts surrounding the station still bear witness.

To go with their new railway the H&M engaged James Pigott Pritchett to design an impressive station. Part was completed in time for the 1847 opening and the remainder in 1850, the year in which the LYR-sponsored Huddersfield & Sheffield Junction Railway opened another scenic route through the high country to Barnsley, plus a branch to Holmfirth. The station at Huddersfield became a joint LYR and LNWR (as successors to the H&M) activity and was given a new roof in 1884-86 when a partial roof collapse killed three workmen.

Well-positioned for the town, Huddersfield station comprises a 416 ft frontage leading to the Up platform. A Down island is reached by subway and beyond lies the former goods yard. There stand a former stone warehouse, and another in red and blue brick with capstan-served wagon hoist, rising four storeys, and with its pump

house not far away.

The J. P. Pritchett building comprises a two-storey entrance portico in the Corinthian style with six front and two side columns. Eight-columns sections on either side are then completed by the four-column end pavilions, the one at the north end bearing the H&M coat of arms and the one at the south those of the LYR. These are repeated in the ticket hall which also has a wall mural. The station, which lies between the 663-yard Huddersfield Viaduct to the north and the 243-yard Gledholt North and South Tunnels at the other end, has main and subsidiary roof spans, and a signal box on the Down island.

A view of the Huddersfield station frontage from the south end pavilion.

HULL PARAGON

Origins: opened 1848, York & North Midland Railway, architect G. T. Andrews; rebuilt 1904, NER, architect William Bell; BR renovation 1979-81.
Location: terminus of lines from Doncaster/Leeds and from Scarborough. 196¾ miles from King's Cross.
Main routes: Hull-King's Cross; cross-Pennine route to Chester and beyond.
Other routes: Hull-Doncaster/ Sheffield; Hull-York; Hull-Scarborough.
Services: InterCity 'Hull Executive' and 'Hull Pullman' to King's Cross; cross-Pennine Sprinters via Manchester to Chester and North Wales; local trains to Doncaster/Sheffield, Leeds, York and Beverley/Bridlington/ Scarborough. 175 trains daily in 1988. Fastest service to London 2 hours 35 minutes (76.2 mph), 1938 4 hours (49.1 mph).
Platforms: 7, including one bay.
Facilities: ticket and information centre, refreshments, bookstall, parcels, left luggage, parking, car hire, taxis, bus and coach station adjoining (including Humberlink and North Sea Ferry services).

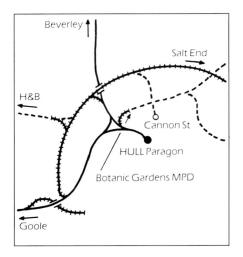

Of special interest: 1848 Andrews station frontage and Paragon Hotel, 1904 booking hall and timber buildings, ex-H&B docks route, Botanic Gardens motive power depot.

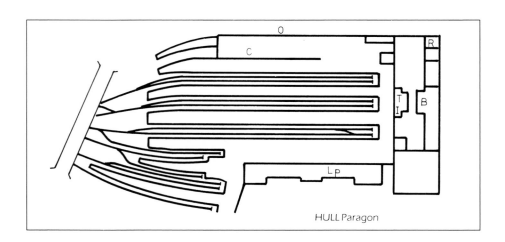

HULL Paragon

Sprinter and Pacer units, here standing side by side, work most of the services to and from Hull.

A Hull City Council plaque on the BR station at Hull reads: 'Paragon Station, opened 1848, substantially enlarged to a design by William Bell 1904, was the principal passenger station of the North Eastern Railway which, with its docks, cartage, hotel and shipping interests, was a major local employer.' The station took over from an 1840 one built by Hull's first railway, the Hull & Selby. It was the work of G. T. Andrews whose classical facade, with its supplementary terrace and end buildings, can still be seen on the south side, and who added an hotel nearby.

To Hull's original services from Leeds/York and the Scarborough line more traffic was added with the opening of the Withernsea (1854) and Hornsea (1864) branches, with increased shipping activity and with new routes from York and Doncaster, until rebuilding became essential and was carried out in 1903-04. This increased the parallel platforms to ten (plus four excursion platforms) and altered the emphasis to the present frontage where a new booking hall and service buildings were provided. The rival Hull & Barnsley Railway was merged with the NER in 1922 and its trains transferred from Cannon Street to Paragon two years later. The H&B route was then closed in 1955, with the Withernsea, Hornsea and Market Weighton lines following in the '60s.

The Hull station approach from Ferensway, with its contrast between the attractive hotel and the ugly Paragon House, leads via the great tiled booking hall to a spacious transverse concourse. This area was renovated in 1979-81 and now houses a modernistic travel centre in addition to contrasting wooden buildings surviving from the 1904 changes. Two transverse roof spans cover this area which leads to the surviving platforms and their five parallel spans, two of which now protect only a car parking area.

Although Hull's coastal branches, the dock lines, Riverside Quay passenger station and the New Holland ferry have all gone, the former H&B route round the city to Salt End is still in use for freight, and the surviving passenger routes are busy. The station is conveniently located in relation to the city and is next to the bus station.

The original 1848 station frontage at Hull Paragon, the work of architect G. T. Andrews.

INVERNESS

Origins: opened 1855, Inverness & Nairn Railway; BR refurbishment.

Location: northern terminus of routes from Perth and Aberdeen; interchange point with lines to Wick/Thurso and Kyle of Lochalsh. 581¼ miles from King's Cross via Larbert.

Main routes: Edinburgh/Glasgow-Perth-Inverness; Inverness-Wick/Thurso and Kyle of Lochalsh.

Other routes: Inverness-Aberdeen.

Services: InterCity services to King's Cross and Euston including sleepers, the 'Highland Chieftain', 'Royal Highlander' and 'Clansman'. ScotRail Expresses Edinburgh/Glasgow-Perth-Inverness, services to Wick/Thurso including the 'Orcadian' and Kyle of Lochalsh including 'Hebridean Heritage' with observation saloon, local trains to Aberdeen. 50 trains daily in 1988. Fastest service to London 8 hours 5 minutes (71.9 mph), 1938 12 hours 15 minutes (47.4 mph).

Platforms: 7, including one bay.

Facilities: Travel Centre, refreshments, bookstall, parcels, left luggage, car hire, parking in former goods yard, local buses pass.

Of special interest: all radiating routes; Ness, Tomatin and Culloden

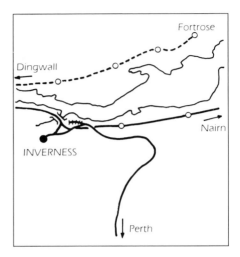

viaducts on Perth line; 1855-59 Station Hotel; 1873-75 HR offices; two I&AJR plaques; station bell; BR maintenance depot on former HR Lochgorm Works site.

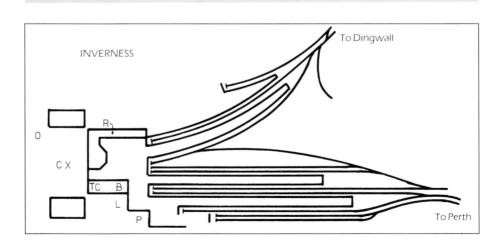

A Class '47' stands on a Perth train at Inverness in 1988.

There is a sense of drama on the rail approach to Inverness, whether along the shoreline from the Nairn direction or descending from the Grampian summits via the great Tomatin and Culloden viaducts. The station itself is no let-down, and the feeling stayed alive as trains left over the gracious River Ness bridge to cover another 161½ miles to Wick or 82¼ miles across to Kyle of Lochalsh on the west coast. Severe floods in 1989 swept away the 1862 Ness Viaduct, but it is being rebuilt. Inverness itself is full of interest and the BR station lies close to its centre.

The Great North of Scotland Railway exhausted its fund in reaching Keith and it was left to local interests to give Inverness its first line, a 15 mile route to Nairn which was opened on 5 November 1855. Although this subsequently became a through route to the south via Aberdeen, its circuitous nature prompted calls for a more direct line, opened from Forres to Perth in 1863 and shortened by 26 miles in 1898. By this time the lines to the far north and to Skye were also open and the various independent concerns had merged into the Highland Railway.

Inverness was the focal point of the Highland Railway system. Outside the station is the former HR headquarters building with what used to be a railway hotel opposite. Then comes an attractively modernized concourse with a Travel Centre and other facilities and with the station administration block along one wall at first floor level. Beyond lie the seven platforms with short, staggered roof sections and with two cast iron commemorative notices of the Inverness & Aberdeen Junction Railway, a station bell of 1858, and the HR coat of arms in stone.

The Inverness platforms are in 'vee' formation, the two for Dingwall trains and No 7 bay curving round ready for their route northwards. From the end of these a connecting line to the Perth route also serves the maintenance depot and stabling sidings, once the site of the Highland's locomotive works. Through trains used to use this route and then reverse into the station before their onward journey. On the Down side of the station the former goods shed survives and there are lines for Motorail loadings.

An ornate plaque on Inverness station commemorating the completion of the through route to Aberdeen.

IPSWICH

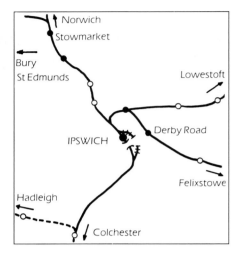

Origins: opened 1860, Great Eastern Railway, engineer Robert Sinclair; Down island platform added 1883.

Location: London-Norwich main line, junction with East Suffolk and Felixstowe lines. 68¼ miles from Liverpool Street.

Main routes: Liverpool Street-Ipswich-Norwich, and Harwich Parkeston Quay/Ipswich-Birmingham/North West via Peterborough.

Other routes: Ipswich-Felixstowe, Ipswich-Saxmundham/Lowestoft and Ipswich-Cambridge.

Services: electric InterCity services Liverpool Street-Ipswich-Norwich, including the 'East Anglian'. Sprinters Harwich Parkeston Quay/Ipswich to Birmingham/Blackpool/Liverpool/Manchester, including the 'Loreley'. Local dmu service on Felixstowe branch (calling at Derby Road, Ipswich), to Saxmundham/Lowestoft on the East Suffolk Line, and to Cambridge via Bury St Edmunds. 168 trains daily in 1988. Fastest service to London 1 hour 5 minutes (63 mph), 1938 1 hour 20 minutes (51.2 mph).

Platforms: 4, including one bay.

Facilities: ticket office, Travel Centre, refreshments, bookstall, parcels, left luggage, car hire, parking, taxis, local buses.

Of special interest: 1860 station buildings, footbridge and Down side canopy, fuelling depot, station plaques, Cliffe Quay freight branch.

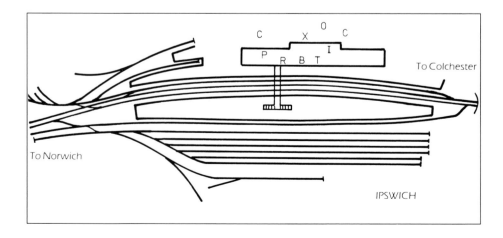

The 1860 main buildings at Ipswich station. These once housed the Ipswich District offices.

Ipswich remains a traditional station but that in no way detracts from its modern role as an interchange point between the Class 86-hauled InterCity services on the electrified main line and its local routes to Felixstowe, Lowestoft and Cambridge. Trains on the two eastern routes use either the Up side country-end bay or the adjacent No 2 platform, while those on the inland route use the far side of the Down island to facilitate interchange with the main-line services. Dmus were still handling the local services in 1988 although Sprinters were at work on the trains to the North West via Ely.

Ipswich station, some way from the town centre but well served by buses and taxis, stands in Ranelagh Street near the River Orwell. The main buildings front the Up platform and were designed by Robert Sinclair, reflecting the Italianate influences which had appeared at other ECR/GER stations of the 1860 period. They consist of a two-storey main block, in cream brick with red brick decoration, with projecting entrance section and a variety of chimney structures. A very traditional footbridge, decorated to show it at its best, then leads to the Down island where a section of wooden ridge and furrow canopy, complete with valances, has survived the intrusion of overhead wiring masts. The station site is bounded by the 361-yard Ipswich Tunnel to the south and by a traction stabling and refuelling depot to the west.

When the Eastern Counties Railway ran out of funds after reaching Colchester, Ipswich interests helped to create the Eastern Union Railway which bridged the gap with a line opened from Colchester to a terminus south of the present tunnel on 15 June 1846. It was linked with Bury St Edmunds the following year and with Norwich in 1849. A new station on the present site then became operational from 1 July 1860 with the old location becoming a locomotive depot. The new station was originally a long, single platform affair, similar to the one at Cambridge, but a Down island was added to create the present layout in 1883.

The north end of Ipswich station with an East Suffolk line dmu standing in the bay platform.

LANCASTER CASTLE

Origins: opened 1846, Lancaster & Carlisle Railway, architect Sir William Tite; extended 1858 and 1906.

Location: West Coast Main Line, just south of junction with Morecambe branch. 230 miles from Euston.

Main routes: West Coast Main Line, Manchester-Glasgow and Manchester/Preston-Barrow, South/South West-Scotland, and Leeds-Morecambe.

Other routes: Lancaster-Carnforth, and Morecambe branch.

Services: WCML InterCity services Euston/Coventry/Birmingham-Lancaster/Carlisle/Scotland, including the 'Clansman', 'Royal Scot' and 'Night Caledonian' sleeper; also Poole/Brighton/Penzance/Paignton-Scotland including the 'Wessex', 'Sussex', 'Devon' and 'Cornish' 'Scots'; and Manchester-Barrow/Glasgow. Leeds-Lancaster-Morecambe Sprinters plus local Morecambe branch services and Preston/Lancaster-Carnforth/Barrow trains. 156 trains daily in 1988. Fastest service to London 3 hours 4 minutes (75 mph), 1938 4 hours 29 minutes (47.8 mph).

Platforms: 5, including 2 bays.

Facilities: tickets and information, refreshments, parcels and left luggage,

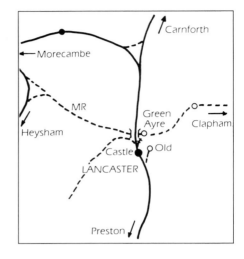

parking, taxis, local buses pass, Seaways bus link with Isle of Man steamers.

Of special interest: original Down side buildings, bay platform buffer stops, Up island milepost, Lune bridge.

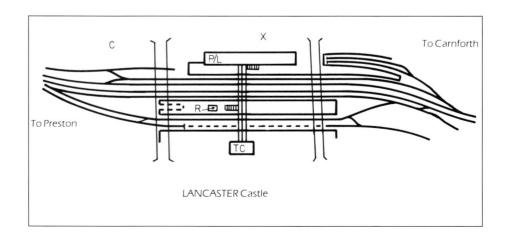

LANCASTER Castle

The 1846 Down side buildings at Lancaster were the work of Sir William Tite for the Lancaster & Carlisle Railway.

Lancaster was connected to the railway system on 25 June 1840 when the Lancaster & Preston Junction Railway opened its line south to meet the North Union Railway at Preston. This gave Lancashire's historic county town a rail route through to London and a station at the top of Penny Street. Initially called Lancaster Greaves, and later 'Old', this became potentially redundant six years later when the Lancaster & Carlisle Railway opened northwards on 22 September 1846. The new railway left the L&PJ just south of Old station and passed west of the castle hill from which its station took its name.

The Old Station ceased to deal with passengers from 1 August 1849 but continued to serve as a goods depot until 1967. A year earlier Lancaster's Green Ayre station had lost its passenger trains on what had once been an important Midland Railway line from Clapham to Lancaster, and on to Morecambe and Heysham. These two 1848-49 routes east and west from Lancaster have both closed,

but the LNWR route to Morecambe, and a continuation over the MR to Heysham, survive. A daily passenger service operates between Lancaster's bay platforms and Morecambe, and a bus service connects with the Isle of Man steamers at Heysham.

The elegant station produced in 1846 for the Lancaster & Carlisle Railway was the work of Sir William Tite. Matching its castle neighbour, the pleasant stone buildings with gabled sections flanking the entrance were extended at the south end in 1858 by the addition of an elaborate tower block. The Up side buildings were added in the first years of the present century. These now house the ticket office and are linked by footbridge with the centre island and the Down platform which has a double bay at the north end. A notice here forbids trains to stand with the hydraulic buffer stops of the bay platforms compressed and there is a period destination board post nearby.

Lancaster station is followed by the three-span Carlisle Bridge across the River Lune.

LEEDS

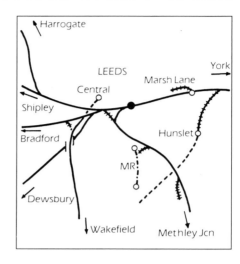

Origins: new BR station 1967 on Leeds City site.

Location: terminus for East Coast Main Line West Riding services and interchange point with through cross-Pennine services. 185¼ miles from King's Cross.

Main routes: Leeds-King's Cross; Newcastle-Leeds-Liverpool; North East-South West route; Leeds-Morecambe/Carlisle, Hull-Leeds-North Wales and York/Scarborough-Liverpool.

Other routes: Leeds to Selby, to Doncaster/Scunthorpe, Ilkley, Sheffield, Skipton, Harrogate/York, and Manchester Victoria (via Huddersfield and via Halifax).

Services: InterCity services to King's Cross via Doncaster including the 'Yorkshire Pullmans' and 'Bradford Executive'; also on routes to South/South West/Wales via Birmingham, including the 'Armada', 'Devonian' and 'Northumbrian'. Cross-Pennine Sprinters Scarborough/York to Manchester and Liverpool, and Hull-Chester/North Wales; also Newcastle-Liverpool and Leeds-Morecambe/Carlisle services. Local trains on the Goole line, to Doncaster/Scunthorpe, to Sheffield (via Barnsley and via Wakefield), to York (via Church Fenton and via Harrogate), to Marsden/Manchester, to Skipton and on the Ilkley branch. 675 trains daily in 1988. Fastest service to London 2 hours 19 minutes (79.8 mph), 1938 2 hours 44 minutes (67.8 mph).

Platforms: 10, including 5 bays.

Facilities: ticket office, Travel Centre, platform information point, refreshments, bookstall, shops, parcels, left luggage, car hire, parking nearby, taxis, local buses.

Of special interest: traffic working, Queens Hotel, remains of Central and Wellington Street stations, Middleton Railway.

The route to Leeds is the first to receive major benefits from the electrification of the East Coast Main Line. Power was switched on at the end of 1988 followed by crew training to permit the progressive introduction of electric services in 1989. The Class '91' locomotives initially worked with HST sets as part of the transition to the new InterCity 225 trains which have the world's greatest power unit output coupled with the lowest track loading of any high speed train. The 1989 timetables reflected these changes with a 2 hours 5 minutes timing to London for the Up 'Yorkshire Pullman', an average of 88.9 mph, while a trial IC225 trip on 17 September reached a top speed of 161.7 mph.

On 1 May 1967 the long-discussed idea of a single railway station for Leeds at last became a reality. The scheme involved extensive alterations to the approach lines to the west but has proved amply justified in terms of passenger convenience and travel numbers. Overall rail travel in the Leeds area has grown dramatically as a result of investment by the West Yorkshire Passenger Transport Executive in stations, trains and other facilities, and further growth will follow the electrification of the Eastern Region rail route to King's Cross.

The passenger movements through Leeds are handled at five through and five bay platforms. These deal with the local flows on the seven lines radiating from Leeds, plus the InterCity services and the cross-Pennine Sprinters. Traffic is exchanged between the Chester-Hull and Liverpool-York/Scarborough routes of the latter and with the trains to and from Bradford, Halifax, Blackpool, Morecambe, Carlisle, Sheffield, Huddersfield, Doncaster, Ilkley, Harrogate and Scunthorpe. Leeds station is conveniently situated on the south side of the city centre, it has extensive customer care facilities, and there is a host of ancillary railway activities in the area including Neville Hill maintenance depot, Stourton Freightliner terminal and a variety of freight depots and sidings.

The first railway to serve Leeds derived from a scheme to give the city a link to the port of Hull. This was the Leeds & Selby Railway whose line was opened as early as 22 September 1834 and carried passengers to the River Ouse at Selby where a steamer completed the journey on to Hull. The Leeds terminus was in Marsh Lane on a site now occupied by a cement terminal.

Leeds was linked with York via Milford in 1839 and two years later got its first route to London when the North Midland Railway's trains started using a new terminus at Hunslet Lane which opened on 1 July 1840, and was subsequently used by the trains of the Manchester & Leeds Railway. Neither Marsh Lane nor Hunslet was well sited, however, and they became redundant with the opening of the first station in the Wellington Street area in 1846 when services commenced on the Leeds & Bradford Railway's route via Shipley on 1 July and those on earlier lines transferred to this more central location.

A second main station for Leeds came into use during 1849 handling the Harrogate line trains of the Leeds & Thirsk company and those of the LNWR from Manchester. Completion of the new terminus then got bogged down in intercompany rivalry, and it finally emerged as the home of services on the Lancashire & Yorkshire and Great Northern routes from 1854.

The railway network of Leeds was further consolidated when the little-used 1834 route into Marsh Lane was extended west to create a direct through line. The work and expense involved were considerable because of the high-level course taken

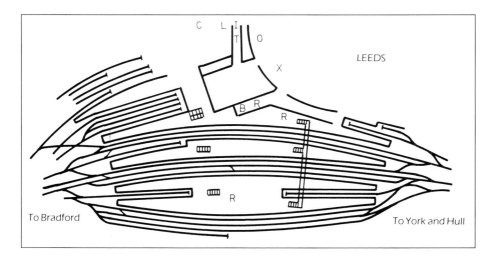

Pacers and Sprinters are a marked feature of Leeds station, many operated on behalf of the West Yorkshire PTE.

The approach to the present Leeds station. The Queens Hotel stands to the right.

Leeds Station, looking east over the 1869 section which created the through east-west route.

and the need to cross both waterways and church grounds, but the line was ready for use in 1869 and revolutionized the train service pattern of the area. It brought with it a new station, appropriately named Leeds New, sited south of Wellington and a joint venture by the LNW and North Eastern railways. From 1938 the Wellington and New stations were linked as Leeds City and were then finally united in the BR scheme which produced today's station and closed Central from 1 May 1967.

The present Leeds station straddles the River Aire and its parcels lines occupy the former Wellington Street site. The main station is approached via a spacious concourse which then leads to the principal platform, No 5, the subway leading to the other platforms, and the west-end bays used for local services. There are two islands beyond the main platform, with Up and Down goods lines round the outside of the station. All platform lines are bi-directional, No 6 being the Down Main, and the Up Main passing between platforms 8 and 9.

Approaching Leeds from the south and west, some of the remains of the bridge leading to the former Central station can still be seen and there are still signs of the old Wellington Street in the car park area. This lies behind the great, classical Queens Hotel, built by the LMS in 1937 and standing next to the modern BR station. Arches, bridges and viaducts abound in the Leeds area and the privately preserved 1758 Middleton Railway acts as a reminder, not only of the first railway to be authorized by Act of Parliament, but also of the Leeds tradition of private locomotive building.

LEICESTER LONDON ROAD MR/LMS/LMR

Origins: built 1892, Midland Railway, architect Charles Trubshaw; refurbished by BR.

Location: former Midland main line, junction with Birmingham line. 99 miles from St Pancras.

Main routes: St Pancras-Leicester-Sheffield and Birmingham-East Anglia.

Other routes: Coventry-Leicester-Nottingham.

Services: InterCity services Sheffield/Derby/Nottingham-Leicester-St Pancras, including the 'Nottingham Executive' and 'Master Cutler'. Cross-country Sprinters Birmingham-Leicester-Cambridge/Norwich and local services to Birmingham, Coventry and Nottingham/Lincolnshire. 135 trains daily in 1988. Fastest service to London 1 hour 16 minutes (80 mph), 1938 1 hour 39 minutes (60 mph).

Platforms: 4.

Facilities: ticket office, Travel Centre, refreshments, bookstalls, parcels, left luggage, car park, car hire, taxis, local buses nearby.

Of special interest: station frontage, former goods yard buildings

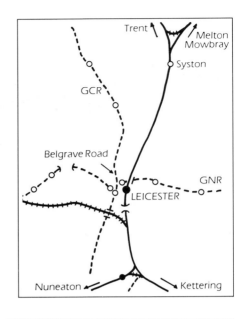

(Down side, north end), MR trespass notice.

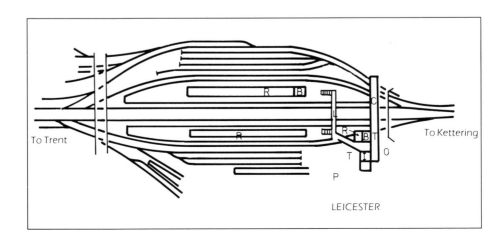

LEICESTER

Charles Trubshaw produced a highly ornate design for the Midland Railway's new Leicester station in 1892.

The Leicester & Swannington Railway is numbered among Britain's railway pioneers and opened the first section of its line, from Leicester to Bagworth, on 17 July 1832. In the following year the Midland Counties Railway issued its plans for routes from Derby, Nottingham, and Pinxton and on to join the London & Birmingham at Rugby. It reached Leicester from Trent on 5 May 1840 and opened the Rugby portion on 30 June of that year. As part of the Midland Railway, the MCR system was linked to London from 1857 and direct to St Pancras from 1867-68. The London & North Western, Great Northern and Great Central companies all opened lines to Leicester but only three of the former eight radiating routes now carry passengers.

The Leicester & Swannington had a station of sorts on the west side of Leicester and although this was replaced after the 1893 rerouting of the L&S, its successor lasted only until 1928. The original, substantial single-platform MCR station was located in Campbell Street, but in 1892 the present site in London Road, about ½ mile from the city centre, was brought into use. The GNR's Belgrave Road closed on 29 April 1957 and the ex-GCR Central station on 5 May 1969.

Architect Charles Trubshaw produced a striking building on the London Road station site, consisting of a long frontage in terracotta, with double arrival and departure arches and a hectagonal clock tower. Urns surmount the long parapet and there is a considerable amount of carved decoration throughout. Beyond the *porte-cochère* the modest circulating area houses the main station facilities and has been remodelled in green and cream, a theme that is continued on the new platform buildings and their canopies. There are left luggage lockers on the wooden footbridge which retains its iron roof spandrels and leads to the two island platforms.

A period wooden awning covers the Down side parcels dock and a wooden passageway leads from the footbridge to the GPO premises. Disused carriage cleaning sidings stand beyond the Up island and there is an 1893 MR trespass notice on the approach past the Area Manager's building.

LEWES

Origins: opened 1889, London, Brighton & South Coast Railway.
Location: junction of London-Eastbourne and Brighton-Hastings routes. 50¼ miles from Victoria.
Main routes: Victoria-Eastbourne/Hastings and Brighton-Eastbourne/Hastings.
Other routes: Brighton-Seaford.
Services: main-line services Victoria to Eastbourne and Hastings via Lewes and connecting there with local Brighton-Seaford emus. Latter alternate with Brighton-Eastbourne/Hastings trains. 152 trains daily in 1988. Fastest service to London 1 hour 3 minutes (47.9 mph), 1938 1 hour 1 minute (49.4 mph).
Platforms: 5.
Facilities: tickets and information, refreshments, bookstall, parcels and left luggage, parking, taxis.
Of special interest: ornate main station buildings with many typical LB&SCR features, traces of former routes on Down side, Seaford line and shipping activity at Newhaven.

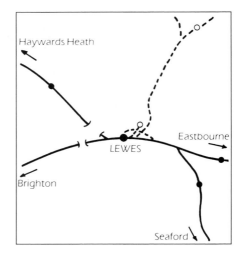

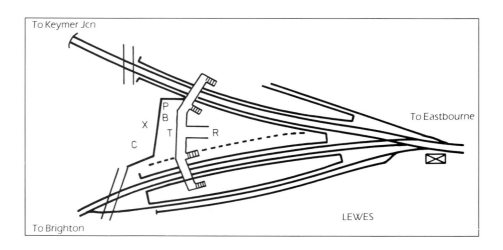

The highly decorated 1889 London, Brighton & South Coast Railway station buildings at Lewes.

This pleasant Sussex town is the meeting point for the former London, Brighton & South Coast Railway lines from the Brighton and London directions, which then separate again east of Lewes to continue their course to Seaford and Hastings. The station used also to have a route north to Horsted Keynes and Eridge but, despite losing this in 1969, the pleasant location remains busy and handles a considerable volume of interchange between the four radiating lines.

The first Lewes station, in Friar's Walk, was opened when the Brighton, Lewes & Hastings Railway's line arrived from the east on 8 June 1846, and then pushed on to Hastings from separate platforms a few days later. Further platform accommodation was added when the line from Keymer Junction arrived in 1847, but ten years later Lewes got a new station in place of the previous jumble of platforms. This in turn was replaced, on 17 June 1889, by the present complex which was provided with easier curves and better platform interchange, all reached via an imposing entrance block on the overbridge above.

The 1889 station buildings are very 'Brighton' in style, sporting the typical LB&SCR wooden lantern above a hipped roof and surrounded by plenty of decoration — a parapet, acorn finials and rounded chimneys. The single-storey main block is in cream brick and, again, well decorated, especially around the window arches. Beyond the ticket hall an angled footbridge leads to the central 'vee' platform and to the outer ones beyond.

One of the coastal line platforms has now been filled in but its position is still apparent. Similarly, the observer can spot the course of the original line towards Uckfield and of the elevated route above it taken by the line from Friar's Walk, which came to be used for goods traffic.

Lewes signal box stands east of the station and has a panel covering the area out to Glynde, Newhaven Town, Cooksbridge and Falmer. East of Lewes the Brighton route departs via the 107-yard Kingston Tunnel and that to Victoria via the 396-yard Lewes Tunnel. The basic train service pattern is of Victoria-Eastbourne/Hastings services with connection into the Brighton-Seaford ones.

A Seaford-Brighton train at the junction of the Brighton and Victoria lines east of Lewes station.

LINCOLN CENTRAL

Origins: opened 1848, Great Northern Railway, architect possibly Lewis Cubitt.

Location: junction of former GN&GER Joint line with lines to Cleethorpes and Nottingham. 136½ miles from King's Cross.

Main routes: Cleethorpes-Lincoln-Nottingham-Derby-Birmingham, and Peterborough-Doncaster.

Other routes: Lincoln-Sheffield.

Services: the 'Humber-Lincs' HST service to and from King's Cross plus links provided with the East Coast Main Line at Newark by some of the Cleethorpes-Birmingham route trains. Peterborough-Lincoln-Doncaster/Sheffield trains plus some Sleaford/Boston/Skegness workings. 81 trains daily in 1988. Fastest service to London 1 hour 59 minutes (68.9 mph), 1938 2 hours 24 minutes via Grantham (54.2 mph).

Platforms: 7, including 4 bays (not normally used).

Facilities: tickets and information, refreshments plus small bookstall, parcels, left luggage, parking, taxis, city and Roadcar buses nearby.

Of special interest: traditional signal box and crossing gates, St Marks

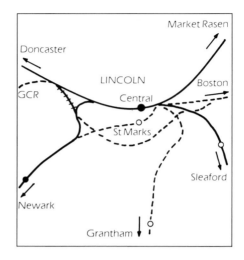

station building, LNER footpath dedication notice, ex-MR war memorial repositioned and re-dedicated 1985 following concentration of services on Central.

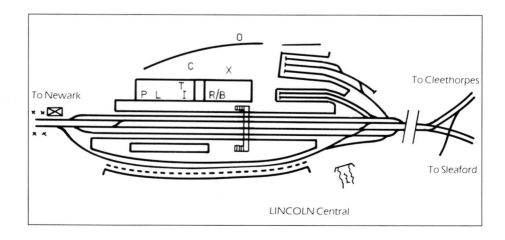

LINCOLN Central

High Street signal box controls the westbound exit from Lincoln and the gates on the busy road of the same name.

Its High Street position makes the former Central station at Lincoln extremely convenient, but in the days when it had a level crossing at both ends, and there was another one at St Marks station just down the road, traffic conditions often became chaotic. Now the Sincil Bank crossing has been replaced by a flyover and St Marks closed, its single-storey classical building with Ionic columns boarded up and part of the site allocated for a new magistrates' court.

St Marks had been Lincoln's first station, opening when the Midland Railway trains from Newark began running on 3 August 1846. Central opened two years later, on 17 October 1848, when the Great Northern Railway's original route from Boston arrived. Lines from Market Rasen (1848), Gainsborough and Retford (1849-50), Grantham/Doncaster (1867), Spalding (1882) and Chesterfield (1897) followed, Lincoln eventually becoming a major junction on the GN&GER Joint line, with an avoiding line and a marshalling yard at Pyewipe.

Following the closure of St Marks, trains were concentrated on the ex-GNR station which had already lost its Boston, Grantham and Chesterfield routes and no longer uses either the east-end bays or the former outer platform. The surviving working layout consists of just the main platform with a footbridge over four running lines to an island platform, all five

tracks then reducing to two to pass the attractive little High Street signal box which controls the massive wooden gates across the main road.

The 1848 station building is an impressive affair with a two-storey main section with crenellated tower, tall chimneys and gables, and a steeply pitched roof. Possibly the work of Lewis Cubitt, its stonework and Tudor style harmonize well with a city so powerfully overlooked by the high cathedral. It does not seem out of place with the nearby church and a landscaped frontage has added to the station's appearance. Within, a through service to London and a good pattern of Sprinter services have replaced the days of LNER 4-4-0s bringing Lincolnshire folk to market or taking them for a day's outing to 'Skeggy'.

The main buildings at Lincoln's former Great Northern station may have been designed by Lewis Cubitt.

LIVERPOOL LIME STREET

Origins: 1867-74 replacement of 1836 and 1849 stations, London & North Western Railway, engineers William Baker and Francis Stevenson.

Location: Lime Street is the terminus of the ex-LNWR main line from Euston via Crewe, and of the original 1830 line from Manchester. With Central, Moorfields and James Street it forms the 'Loop' of the Merseyrail Wirral lines, while Central and Moorfields also deal with Northern line trains. 194¼ miles from Euston.

Main routes: Liverpool-Euston, and to South West/South Wales and Poole; Liverpool-York-Scarborough/Newcastle; Liverpool-Sheffield-East Anglia.

Other routes: Lime Street to Allerton/Crewe, Warrington, Wigan/Preston/Blackpool, and to Manchester Victoria. Merseyrail stations to Wirral and Northern lines.

Services: Lime Street — electrically-hauled InterCity trains to Euston, including the 'Merseyside Pullman'; also services to the South West, South Wales and Poole via Birmingham. Sprinters via Manchester Piccadilly and Sheffield to East Anglia. Fast service to Manchester Victoria, to York/Scarborough/Newcastle, and

local and semi-fast trains to Wigan/Preston/Blackpool, plus locals to Warrington and Allerton/Crewe. Merseyrail Wirral line emus to New Brighton, West Kirkby and Hooton (for Chester) from Moorfields, Lime Street, Central and James Street; Northern line trains from Central and Moorfields to Hunts Cross/Southport, Ormskirk and Kirkby. Lime Street (BR) — 316 trains daily in 1988; Central and Moorfields (Northern line) — 370 trains call at each; Central, Lime Street, Moorfields and James Street — 385 Wirral line trains call at each. Fastest service to London 2 hours 30 minutes (77.3 mph), 1938 3 hours 20 minutes (58 mph).

Platforms: 10.

Facilities: ticket office, Travel Centre, refreshments, bookstall, parcels and left luggage, taxis, parking nearby, local bus routes adjacent.

Of special interest: James Street and waterfront, former Exchange station (Moorfields), Edge Hill and 1830 line to Manchester, railway hotels, Lime Street's 1984 concourse remodelling, and clock by Joyce of Whitchurch.

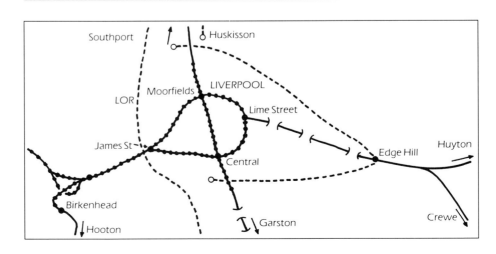

The Down side of Lime Street station showing the substantial roof support pillars.

From the InterCity trains approaching Edge Hill station and the final run into Liverpool's Lime Street terminus it is possible to see the cutting which took the original Liverpool & Manchester Railway trains to its 1830 Crown Street terminus. This was soon to prove inadequate, which led to the building of a cavernous extension from Edge Hill into Lime Street. The station there opened on 15 August 1836 and less than a year later was handling the Grand Junction Railway services that linked Liverpool with Birmingham and London. The first Grand Junction locomotive works was located at Edge Hill and the GJR's successor, the London & North Western Railway, opened a docks branch from that point in 1866. By that time Lime Street had already been enlarged, and by 1885 its extra routes and traffic had necessitated the quadrupling of its approach lines.

Access to Liverpool from the northern parts of Lancashire was achieved by an

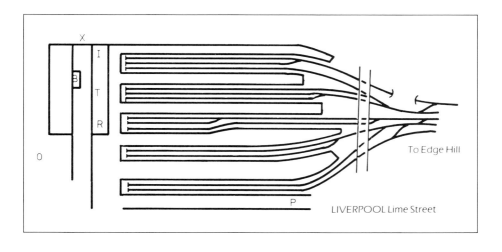

A view across the modern frontage of Lime Street to the former North Western Hotel building.

uneasy partnership between the Lanca-shire & Yorkshire and East Lancashire railways. A terminus for the former's line from Wigan was opened in Great Howard Street in 1848 and was used by the ELR's Ormskirk trains from 1849. The line was extended one year later to a terminus designed by Sir John Hawkshaw which, in turn, was replaced by a new Exchange station on the same site in 1884-88. This was closed in 1977 under the major revision of the rail network in central Liverpool, but the former hotel survives, still carrying the legend 'Exchange Station' and a plaque to LYR chairman John Pearson, as the Mercury Court commercial accommodation development.

The Cheshire Lines Committee, the instrument of the GN, MS&L and Midland railways for improving access to the North West, reached Brunswick Dock Liverpool in 1864 and extended its route to an imposing new Liverpool Central station ten years later. The CLC then added a route round Liverpool to the expanding dock area north of the city, with a new station at Huskisson Dock opening in 1880 and a new line to Southport in 1885. Population and railway expansion south of the Mersey culminated in the 1886 Mersey Railway line

beneath the river to James Street station, with extension to Central Low Level in 1892. Liverpool's other electric railway, the Liverpool Overhead line from Dingle to Seaforth Sands, had begun operating along its elevated docks route the follow-ing year.

Electrification of the lines north of Liverpool in the 1904-13 period and completion of the Wirral electrification by the LMS in 1938 were to take on a new meaning as part of a Liverpool area trans-portation study of the 1960s. The resultant schemes provided for the concentration of main-line services on Liverpool Lime Street and the extension of the underground system to provide a loop for Wirral line trains and a connection between the services using Central and Exchange stations. Although the stations themselves were casualties of the new plans, modern stations were provided in their stead, along with a new burrowing junction at Birkenhead, improved line capacity under the Mersey, and some extension of the existing electrification.

The rail network of the Liverpool city centre now comprises a 2-mile single line tunnel carrying electric multiple units from the Wirral lines in a clockwise loop through

What is left of the LYR's Exchange station has now become part of a commercial enterprise.

James Street, Moorfields, Lime Street and Central stations and then back under the Mersey. At a higher underground level, the Hunts Cross-Southport emus pass between the rebuilt Central Low Level and the new Moorfields station. All the 'loop' stations have modern ticket offices and lift or escalator links to the equally modern platforms. They give easy access to and from Lime Street main-line station, the Moorfields business area, the shops around Central and the waterside via James Street, where the controlling power box is located.

Lime Street has ten platforms under a 219 ft 1867 span and the 186 ft 1874 roof addition. A concourse passes across the city end of these two great arches which are supported on thick double columns of cast iron. The concourse and its facilities, pleasantly remodelled in a scheme of 1984, contrast with the former North Western Hotel of 1871, a massive block in the French Renaissance style for which the architect was Alfred Waterhouse.

Not far from Lime Street station is the Midland Railway's 1912 Adelphi Hotel, while Moorfields station gives access to the surviving Exchange building and James Street to the Mersey ferries and the

maritime museum. Birkenhead has three surviving stations, Edge Hill is worth visiting and there is much of interest on the rail routes out of Liverpool, especially that of the original Liverpool & Manchester pioneer.

The modern lines of BR/Merseyrail's Moorfields station contrast with those of the former Exchange station beyond.

LONDON BLACKFRIARS

Origins: opened as St Pauls 1886, London, Chatham & Dover Railway, engineer J. W. Barry; rebuilt BR 1972-77.

Location: City of London station on Thameslink route. 52¼ miles from Bedford, ½ mile from Holborn Viaduct.

Main routes: Thameslink Bedford line to Brighton, Purley and Orpington/Sevenoaks. Holborn Viaduct to Orpington/Sevenoaks.

Other routes: Holborn Viaduct to West Sutton.

Services: electric Thameslink trains Bedford-Gatwick/Brighton, Luton-Purley and Cricklewood-Orpington/Sevenoaks. Also emu services ex-Holborn Viaduct to Orpington/Sevenoaks and to West Sutton. 316 trains daily in 1988. Fastest service to Sevenoaks 1 hour (27.5 mph), 1938 same.

Platforms: 5.

Facilities: tickets and information, bookstall, Blackfriars Underground station (Circle and District lines), LT buses pass.

Of special interest: 1863 Blackfriars Railway Bridge by Joseph Cubitt, screen of station bridge over under-

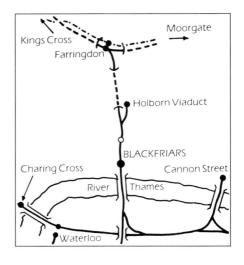

pass, stone quoins from 1886 station, Holborn Viaduct station and remains of Ludgate Hill, Blackfriars Public House, LC&DR coat of arms on Blackfriars Bridge.

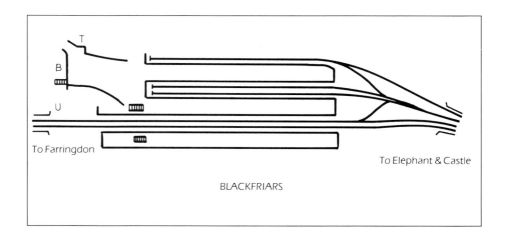

Two Class '319' Thameslink trains stand in the through platforms at Blackfriars beneath its new overall roof.

Located on the north bank of the River Thames immediately after Blackfriars Railway Bridge, this was the first station to bring trains from south of the river into the City of London. Until quite recently Blackfriars was a Monday to Friday station catering just for City commuters, but this has changed with the introduction of the Thameslink services which connect the SR network with the LMR Bedford line via the old cross-London exchange route to Farringdon, where trains now change from third rail current to pantograph collection. For its dual commuter and through service role, Blackfriars has three terminal and two through platforms.

The old London, Chatham & Dover Railway obtained an Act of Parliament for a line from Herne Hill to the Metropolitan at Farringdon Street in 1860 and reached a station on the south bank of the river in 1864. A bridge across the Thames to a temporary station at Ludgate Hill was opened at the end of that year with a permanent station, parts of which can still be seen, following on 1 June 1865. The present Blackfriars site was opened, along with a second bridge, on 10 May 1886,

changing its name from St Pauls to Blackfriars in 1937.

The 1886 station was completely rebuilt between 1972 and 1977, no easy task because of its elevated position on a site frozen solid by use as a cold store. Three bridges over the river and on to Holborn Viaduct, plus the LT lines below, added to the complications. The rebuilding scheme needed an investment of £12 million by the BR and King's College owners, funded from the value of the commercial space created above the entrance area.

The new Blackfriars has a tiled street entrance which incorporates access to the Underground. The office development above has rubber bridge bearings to lessen train vibration effects. A small BR concourse follows at train level and one of its walls houses quoin stones from the old Blackfriars on which were recorded the places it served, from Sheerness and Sevenoaks to Vienna and Venice. The concourse then enlarges to accommodate the ends of the three terminal platforms, the southbound through platform and the subway to the northbound one.

LONDON CANNON STREET

Origins: opened 1866, South Eastern Railway, engineer Sir John Hawkshaw; rebuilt under BR development scheme 1965.

Location: City of London terminus of former SER Kent routes. 74¾ miles from Dover.

Main routes: London to Dartford/ Gravesend/Gillingham/Hayes/Orpington/Barnehurst, plus Margate/Dover/ Folkestone and Hastings in the peaks.

Other routes: Cannon Street-London Bridge shuttle.

Services: patterned electric multiple unit services throughout the day to Dartford, Orpington, Gravesend, Hayes, Barnehurst and London Bridge, plus peak period trains to Hastings and to Sevenoaks/Ashford and Folkestone/Dover/Margate. 255 trains daily in 1988. Fastest service to Dover 1 hour 31 minutes (49.8 mph), 1938 1 hour 43 minutes (43.5 mph).

Platforms: 8.

Facilities: ticket office, City Travel Centre, refreshments, bookstall, shops, taxis, Cannon Street Underground station (Circle and District lines), LT bus routes nearby.

Of special interest: original station walls and towers, concourse plaques, traditional buffer stops.

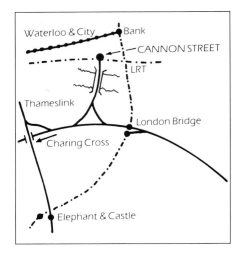

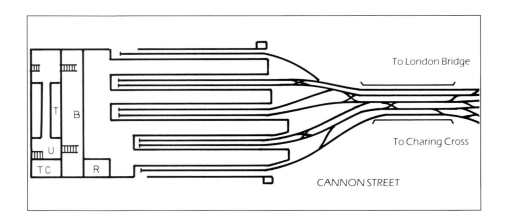

Cannon Street with a full complement of trains and the 1866 walls contrasting with the modern office block.

Cannon Street is closed at weekends, for its main purpose is to serve some 40,000 daily commuters who work in the City of London and live south of the Thames. It is a curiously mixed station, with a huge office block rising above it, the twin walls of the 1866 station on either side terminating in two high towers, and the 70-chain Thames bridge beyond. The station serves the same pattern of stations as Charing Cross, but four of its eight platforms are only used during the peak period.

Like Charing Cross, Cannon Street originated with the SER's Charing Cross Railway project, the City extension from London Bridge being opened on 1 September 1866 and terminating at Sir John Hawkshaw's 700 ft long station raised above Upper Thames Street. The platforms were spanned by a 190 ft crescent roof which rose 100 ft above rail level and whose gable ends stretched between the 120 ft twin towers which stored water for the station's hydraulic systems. The site itself dates back to Roman times and it later accommodated St Mary Bothaw church which was destroyed in the Great Fire of London in 1666. Human

remains and much evidence of earlier human activity were unearthed during the building of the station.

Prior to the 1965 reconstruction, the station approach had been dominated by the five-storey City Terminus Hotel (later the Cannon Street Hotel) which E. M. Barry designed to match its counterpart at Charing Cross. The hotel was burned down in the May 1941 blitz and replaced by the present complex of stairs to the ticket office on a mezzanine floor and then another rise to the main concourse beneath the multi-storey office block. The two platform areas are staggered with a control room between and with some veteran hydraulic buffers beyond the modern access barrier. Then comes the old station shell with the two great towers built to accommodate water reservoirs, restored in 1986 in conjunction with the Railway Heritage Trust and each topped by a weather vane proclaiming the original SER ownership.

Cannon Street trains are controlled by the London Bridge panel, all of them call there and there is a regular shuttle service between the two points.

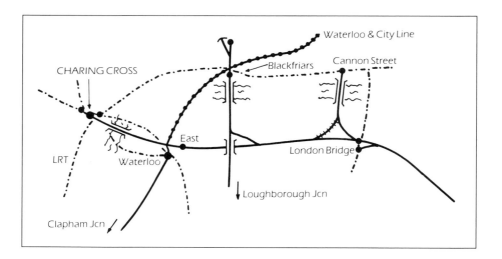

Origins: opened 1864, South Eastern Railway, architect Sir John Hawkshaw; redevelopment commenced 1988.

Location: London North Bank terminus of the former SER main line from Dover and East Kent via Ashford and Tonbridge. 77¼ miles from Dover Priory.

Main routes: Charing Cross-Dover/Margate, and to Ramsgate via Ashford; Charing Cross-Tunbridge Wells/Hastings.

Other routes: South East London routes out to Orpington, Dartford and Gravesend. Charing Cross-London Bridge shuttle.

Services: combined Dover/Margate semi-fast electric services dividing at Ashford. Charing Cross-Sevenoaks/Tonbridge/Ashford/Ramsgate services, and to Tunbridge Wells/Hastings via Tonbridge; also to Liverpool Lime Street. South East London routes services to Bromley North/Hayes/Orpington/Gillingham and Dartford/Gravesend. Interval shuttle service to and from London Bridge. 779 trains daily in 1988. Fastest service to Dover 1 hour 27 minutes (53.3 mph), 1938 1 hour 34 minutes (49.3 mph).

Platforms: 6.

Facilities: tickets and information, refreshments, bookstall, parcels and left luggage, taxis, LT bus routes, Charing Cross Underground station (Jubilee, Northern and Bakerloo lines) and Embankment Underground station (Jubilee, District and Circle lines); near Charing Cross Pier on the Thames; Hungerford Bridge footpath to South Bank.

Of special interest: Eleanor Cross, Hungerford Bridge, station reconstruction.

The early railways into London from the south all had the problem of crossing the Thames in order to gain access to the City and West End. One went underground but the rest had to face up to a bridging task and the high expense of creating a large terminal in already congested areas. Charing Cross was the product of the South Eastern Railway's need to extend westward from London Bridge and get its Kent passengers right into London.

The vehicle used by the SER was the Charing Cross Railway, a scheme approved by Parliament on 8 August 1859 and involving a high-level route forward from London Bridge to a point between Westminster and Waterloo bridges. Negotiations for the purchase of St Thomas's Hospital delayed the project but work eventually started near Hungerford Market in 1862 and included the removal of some 8,000 bodies from the College Burial Ground. Construction was sufficiently advanced for Mid-Kent trains to start using Charing Cross from 11 January 1864, with North Kent and main line trains being added at the beginning of the following May.

The southern approach to Charing Cross is over the Hungerford Bridge which, like the station, was the work of Sir John Hawkshaw. It is a lattice girder bridge with six 154 ft river spans on cast iron piers. Two piers from Brunel's 1845 bridge were used in the new Hungerford works and Hawkshaw also used the chains from the former to complete the Clifton Suspension Bridge at Bristol as a memorial to Brunel. The Hungerford railway bridge, now No 7, initially accommodated four tracks but was subsequently widened to take six at the expense of one of the original footpaths.

At the opposite end of the Charing Cross site the SER wanted a hotel that would support its image as a trunk route to the Continent. It was provided by the architect Edward Middleton Barry who designed a seven-storey building in the French Renaissance style with an elegant interior including lavish public rooms, a domed-ceiling restaurant and wide staircases. The hotel extends across the whole station frontage, with an awning linking the hotel, station and Underground entrances and an ornate ironwork parapet at first floor level.

Although the Charing Cross concourse is modest in size, it is well-equipped and handles some 120,000 passengers daily. The station has six platforms, as originally built, 1 to 3 handling the local services to Dartford, Hayes, Orpington and Sevenoaks, and 4 to 6 dealing with trains to the Medway towns and Kent coast. The ridge and furrow roof is a replacement of the original one, part of which collapsed on 5 December 1905 killing three people in the station and three more in the adjoining Avenue (Players) Theatre.

The station roof is itself being replaced in a current £130 million office development for the station, scheduled for completion in 1989. In essence the scheme is based on piles driven 100 feet into the London clay beneath the station and rising through the platforms to support their 3,500-ton share of a barrel-shaped structure above. The steel structure, with concrete floors, will

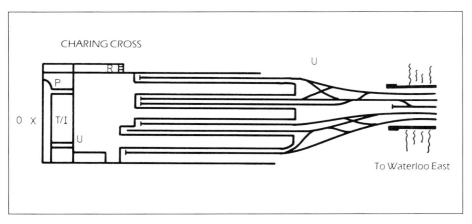

CHARING CROSS

To Waterloo East

By 1988 support piles had been driven through the platforms into the ground beneath Charing Cross station and work had started on the office development above.

The south end of Charing Cross station with a train on the bridge over the Thames.

The concourse at Charing Cross with the hotel above the stopped clock.

hang from huge bow girders which the bell-bottomed piles will raise above the station proper. Within the main scheme a smaller project will provide new BR facilities, including ticket office, Travel Centre and information systems, with the control room and staff accommodation on a raft inside the station. There will also be new shopping facilities at ground level.

In the forecourt of the station complex stands the Eleanor Cross, the point from which Britain measures its road distances. These crosses were originally erected at points at which the body of Eleanor, Edward I's queen, had rested on its journey from Lincoln to Westminster for burial. The original Whitehall cross, demolished in 1647, was replaced by the present Charing Cross replica, the new cross being commissioned by the Charing Cross Hotel Company and designed by E. M. Barry.

LONDON EUSTON

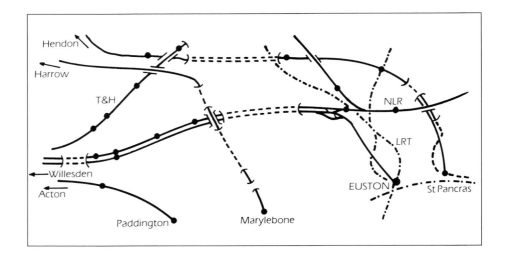

Origins: original station opened 1837, London & Birmingham Railway; various subsequent reconstructions culminating in complete rebuilding by BR in conjunction with the electrification of the West Coast Main Line 1963-68.

Location: London terminus of the West Coast Main Line. 401¼ miles from Glasgow.

Main routes: West Coast Main Line via Trent Valley and via Birmingham. Euston-Rugby-Coventry-Brmingham International-Birmingham New Street/Wolverhampton.

Other routes: Euston-Milton Keynes/Northampton/Birmingham.

Services: West Coast Main Line services to Chester/Holyhead, Manchester/Liverpool, Blackpool, Lancaster/Barrow-in-Furness, Stranraer, and via Carlisle to Glasgow/Edinburgh/Inverness. Sleeper services. Motorail services to Stirling, Carlisle, Edinburgh, Aberdeen and Inverness. Named trains: 'Manchester', 'Merseyside', 'Chester' and 'Lancashire' 'Pullmans', 'Clansman', 'Irish Mail', 'Welsh Dragon', 'Cambrian Coast Express', 'Royal Highlander', 'Night Aberdonian', 'Night Caledonian'. Emu service Euston-Rugby-Coventry-Birmingham/Wolverhampton and Milton Keynes/Northampton/Birmingham. 320 trains daily in 1988. Fastest service to Glasgow Central 5 hours 5 minutes (78.9 mph), 1938 6 hours 30 minutes (61.7 mph).

Platforms: 18.

Facilities: ticket office, Travel Centre and Travel Shop, food court, bookstalls, parcels, left luggage, parking, taxis. Euston Underground station (Northern line) and Euston Square (Circle and Metropolitan lines), LT buses.

Of special interest: entrance lodges of old station in Euston Road, LNWR/LMS war memorial, statue of Robert Stephenson, modern station concourse, LMR Collectors' Corner in nearby Cobourg Street.

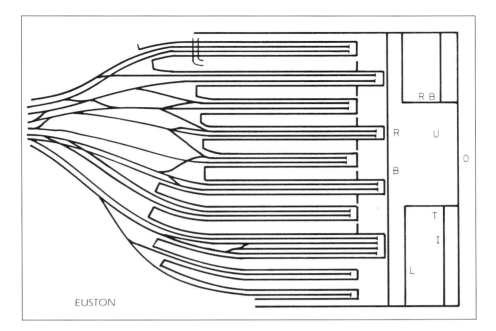

EUSTON

It was fitting that electrification of the West Coast Main Line should be accompanied by a new station for its London terminus, but great was the outcry which greeted the removal of the Doric arch which stood in front of Euston station and symbolized all the pride shown by the London & North Western Railway in what it was pleased to call the Premier Line. Euston had originated with the London & Birmingham Railway which had opened its route as far as Boxmoor on 20 July 1837 and extended to Birmingham in 1838 to join the Grand Junction Railway in creating the first main line to the North. Its London station hardly lived up to its dramatic portico, but its importance has never been in doubt. Its stature would have been even greater if the original discussions about accommodating the infant Great Western Railway had not broken down.

The L&B's original arrival and departure platform accommodation at Euston quickly proved inadequate as more and

The functional lines of the Euston station frontage contrast with the 1930s style of Euston House beyond.

Outside Euston Station stand the LNWR/LMS war memorial and the two lodges of the former station.

more railways were linked with the main line. Further platforms were added in 1840 and a new station building provided before the decade was out. Between these two events the cable haulage used to raise trains from the station to the top of the 1 in 77 Camden Bank was abandoned in favour of the use of a second locomotive. Euston got more platforms and a new roof in 1871-73 and then further platforms 20 years later, eventually bringing the total up to 15. Although suffering from its piecemeal growth, Euston was very under-utilized compared with Liverpool Street or Waterloo, for it had relatively little in the way of surburban commuter business and only a modest train total.

Be all this as it may, the old Euston was swept away in a five-year reconstruction period between 1963 and 1968. This pro-

A mixture of trains and motive power on the eastern side of Euston station in 1988.

duced the present station which the Queen opened on 14 October of the latter year. It is functional rather than good looking but new philosophies on station rebuilding were still emerging at that period and the BRB was permitted no upward commercial development to help defray the cost or permit any non-essential embellishments.

Along the Euston Road the rebuilding of 1963-68 provided space for a series of individual office blocks behind a small park with the new station to the rear. In the centre of this area, Euston Grove leads to a small bus terminal and is flanked by two Portland stone lodges surviving from the old Euston complex. Carrying a great deal of decoration, including the LNWR logo, these also record places served by the Premier Line with the usual generous interpretation of running powers to which pre-grouping companies were prone. The LNWR and LMS war memorial occupies a traffic island beyond the lodges and, on the station side of the office blocks, Carlo Marochetti's 1870 statue of Robert Stephenson stands as a reminder of his work on the design of the original

trainshed.

The new Euston station frontage stretches right across from the LMR offices in Eversholt Street to Melton Street. Its long, two-height, single-storey, glass-dominated design is quite plain and contrasts with the typical 1930s style of the Eversholt Street building which was once the headquarters of the London, Midland & Scottish Railway. The two outer wings of the Euston complex house a variety of retailing activities, with those immediately surrounding the projecting concourse including Travel Shop, Travel Centre and ticket offices to the left and a bookstall and food hall to the right.

The main Euston concourse is surrounded by further ancillary facilities and includes the entrance to the Underground. Its main role is that of passenger circulation to and from the 18 platforms which are reached via gently sloping ramps off a second cross passageway. A large portion of the platform area is covered over with the upper floor accommodating parcels and mail traffic and vehicle parking. Car and taxi access at the front is by ramp.

One of the Class '90' electric locomotives behind the station sign at Euston.

LONDON FENCHURCH STREET

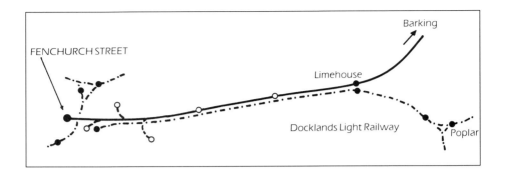

Origins: opened 1841, London & Blackwall Railway; rebuilt 1854, engineer George Berkeley; recent office block development combined with station refurbishment.

Location: City of London terminus of former London, Tilbury & Southend Railway line from Shoeburyness. 39½ miles from Shoeburyness.

Main routes: London to Southend/ Shoeburyness via Basildon and via Tilbury Loop.

Services: semi-fast and all-stations emu services to Southend/Shoebury-ness via Upminster (with Tilbury Riverside connection there) and via Tilbury Town. 229 trains daily in 1988. Fastest service to Southend Central 45 minutes (47.7 mph), 1938 57 minutes (37.6 mph).

Platforms: 4.

Facilities: tickets and information, refreshments, bookstall, parcels, left luggage, near Tower Hill Underground station (District and Circle lines), near Docklands Light Railway station, LT buses pass nearby.

Of special interest: station frontage and refurbishing, former Minories hoist, gantry signal box, Docklands Light Railway.

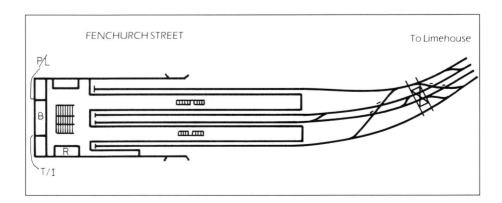

Although Fenchurch Street is close to the heart of the City of London, tucked away amid the financial and shipping houses just north of the Thames, the City shunned the original London & Blackwall Railway which was forced to start from the Minories instead. From there it operated a cable-haulage line designed to compete with the down river steamers and following a route used by today's Docklands Light Railway. The City authorities eventually relented and the L&B line was extended to Fenchurch Street on 2 August 1841 with conversion to conventional haulage coming eight years later when the line was linked with its ECR and NLR neighbours.

The 1841 station by Sir William Tite was rebuilt in 1854 when the iron roof was carried forward to a sizeable, single-arch frontage pediment. Although modest in size, the station came to carry a substantial volume of commuter traffic in the hands of the London, Tilbury & Southend Railway and later the LMS. The Southend excursion business was also significant and the line always had strong shipping connections, including boat trains to and from Tilbury and a special contract for freight from Tilbury Docks to the Commercial Road warehouse.

After many years of service, the 'Tilbury Tanks' began to bow out on 6 November 1961 when the first emu services commenced. More recently Fenchurch Street has experienced another major change as a result of a £28 million develop-

Beyond the Fenchurch Street platforms is the modern station of the Docklands Light Railway.

ment by the BR Property Board and the Norwich Union company. This added a five-storey office block above the station but retained George Berkeley's frontage, the scheme also replacing the outdated interior layout with modern facilities in modern materials.

A ridge and furrow awning stretches across the main station frontage with escalators and stairs then leading up to the four platforms. There is a second entrance in Crutched Friars and between the two the station passes over a cobbled passageway whose name, French Ordinary Court, is a reminder of those who fled the French Revolution. Above, canopies extend along the platforms while beyond them stand the Docklands Light Railway station, the gantry signal box and the old Minories hoist building.

The George Berkeley frontage has been retained in the recent scheme of redevelopment at Fenchurch Street.

LONDON KING'S CROSS

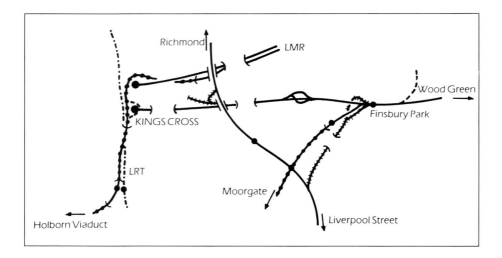

Origins: opened 1852, Great Northern Railway, architect Lewis Cubitt. Remodelled by BR 1973-77.

Location: London terminus of the East Coast Main Line. 393½ miles from Edinburgh and 524 miles from Aberdeen.

Main routes: East Coast Main Line to North East and Scotland, to Leeds and to Humberside.

Other routes: King's Cross to Peterborough, to Letchworth (via Hertford Loop), Royston and Cambridge; also to Welwyn Garden City/Hertford North/Stevenage.

Services: InterCity services over the East Coast Main Line via Peterborough, Grantham and Doncaster to Scotland (Edinburgh/Aberdeen/Inverness) and including the 'Flying Scotsman', 'Talisman', 'Aberdonian' and 'Highland Chieftain'; to the North East including the 'Tees-Tyne Pullman' and 'Cleveland Executive', to Leeds including the 'Yorkshire Pullmans'; and to Humberside including the 'Hull Pullman' and 'Humber-Lincs'. Electric services to Peterborough and on the Cambridge line plus hourly Stevenage and early/late Welwyn Garden City and Hertford North trains. 313 trains daily in 1988. Fastest service to Edinburgh 4 hours 23 minutes (89.8 mph), 1938 6 hours (65.6 mph).

Platforms: 11.

Facilities: ticket office, Travel Centre, refreshments, bookstall, shops, parcels, left luggage, car hire, business parking, taxis, LT bus routes, King's Cross & St Pancras Underground station (Circle, Metropolitan, Piccadilly, Northern and Victoria lines). King's Cross Thameslink station 350 yards away.

Of special interest: station frontage, footbridge clocks and ironwork, former York Road station area.

Compared with the flamboyance of its St Pancras neighbour, King's Cross is a rather prosaic station. Nevertheless, its role as the London terminus of the East Coast Main Line has given it a special standing among London stations, not unconnected with its famous trains like the 'Flying Scotsman' and 'Silver Jubilee', nor unaffected by the romance of Gresley's streamlined 'Pacific' locomotives which were coaled and watered near the entrance to Gasworks Tunnel. After reversing on to their trains, the LNER 'A4s' had to tackle a difficult start over complicated trackwork and then up the 1 in 107 gradient towards Finsbury Park, a task calling for all the skills of the top link drivers at the regulator.

Today's era of High Speed Trains and electrification seems a far cry from the early struggles of the Great Northern Railway. After considerable opposition its main line was opened in 1850 using a terminus at Maiden Lane, King's Cross becoming operational from 14 October 1852 with the completion of the £123,000 station designed by Lewis Cubitt and occupying the site of a former smallpox and fever hospital. This was a two-platform affair with carriage lines between and fronted by a rectangular block housing two eliptical end screens and a central clock tower. The station was covered by a roof supposedly modelled on the Czar's Moscow riding school and the largest of its kind in the world at that time.

The accommodation at King's Cross was

increased several times in the 1862-78 period, the changes including new lines down to the Metropolitan Railway to give the Great Northern access to the City. On the east side of the station a York Road Platform — still visible — was located at the entrance to the tunnel, Down trains rising via Hotel Curve on the west side of the station. The problems of restarting an 'N1' tank from Platform 15 with a train of Quad-Art sets loaded with commuters was another driving skill demanded by King's Cross.

Innovations, such as the first British sleepers and dining cars, plus the competition between the East and West Coast routes to Scotland, kept up the pressure for expansion at King's Cross. Another round in 1892-93 added to the accommodation and provided a third bore for Gasworks Tunnel. This is still in use, its portal in blue engineer's bricks contrasting with the brick and stone used in the original bores. After the First World War more changes, initiated by the Great Northern, were completed by the LNER. Remodelling was then supplemented by the 1932 provision of electric points, colour light signalling and full track circuiting controlled from a 232-mini-lever power frame.

King's Cross welcomed the 'Deltics' in 1962 and prepared for the HSTs by another major remodelling in 1977. This simplified the trackwork of the 'Throat' and closed the east-side bore of Gasworks Tunnel. The diversion of local services to Moorgate

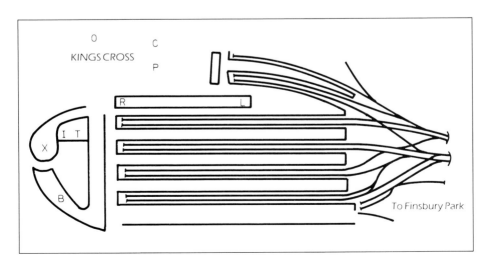

The interior of King's Cross showing the long footbridge and a clock from the Great Northern era.

The exit from King's Cross with the disused original tunnel bore to the right and the old loco shed area to the left.

closed York Road and rendered the Hotel Curve redundant, the suburban station on the west side losing platforms 11 to 15. By this time the frontage had acquired a modern single-storey extension housing shops, a central circulating area, Underground access and a new ticket office and Travel Centre. The latest changes have seen the refurbishing of the suburban station and the reinstatement of platform 11, while forward plans for King's Cross include a redevelopment of 125 acres in the area in a massive scheme that will link the station with St Pancras and provide office, shopping, housing and community facilities.

The frontage extension for King's Cross gave it modern facilities without detracting from the 1852 facade and the tower which houses a Dent clock purchased from the Great Exhibition of 1851. There is a parcels roadway within the plain east side wall and offices along the west side. Between the two, the 800 ft long roof spans rise 71 ft above two sets of four tracks, and a footbridge crosses from one side to the other. With ironwork by Handyside & Co, this also acts as the housing for two more station clocks, the reverses of which betray their GNR origins.

Some 300 yards east of King's Cross main line station, the Thameslink King's Cross station has its entrance in Pentonville Road. On the opposite, west, side is the Great Northern Hotel which was also the work of Lewis Cubitt. The five-storey building in cream brick with stone window dressings and with a curved profile was opened in 1854 and cost £35,000.

Legend has it that Queen Boadicea lies buried beneath King's Cross. If so, the spirit of that enterprising lady will have rejoiced in the railway excitements that have taken place there over the years and not least in the extension of electrification first to Peterborough, then to the West Riding and soon to York, Newcastle and Edinburgh.

The Great Northern Hotel stands between the St Pancras train-shed and the old and new portions of Kings Cross.

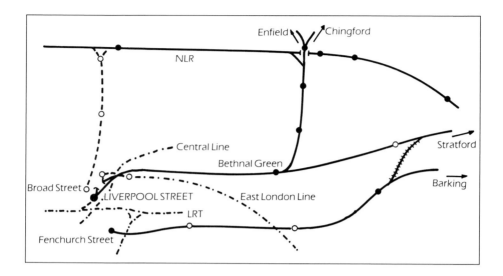

Origins: western side opened 1874-5, eastern 1894, Great Eastern Railway, engineer Edward Wilson. BR redevelopment scheme 1983-92.

Location: London terminus of former GER main lines to Norwich via Ipswich and Kings Lynn via Cambridge. 115 miles from the former, 97 from the latter.

Main routes: Liverpool Street-Cambridge/Kings Lynn and Liverpool Street-Witham/Clacton/ Harwich/ Ipswich/Norwich.

Other routes: Liverpool Street to Shenfield/Southend, to Chingford, to Bishops Stortford/Hertford East and to Enfield Town/Cheshunt.

Services: hourly electrically-hauled main-line service to Ipswich and Norwich, including the 'East Anglian'; also main-line emu services to Harwich and Clacton-on-Sea lines via Chelmsford and Colchester and including London-Amsterdam Euro-City services 'Admiraal de Ruyter' and 'Benjamin Britten'. Also hourly service to Witham and local services to Gidea Park, Shenfield and Southend Victoria. Fast services to Cambridge and Kings Lynn, including the 'Fenman', via the Lea Valley line, plus slower services to Cambridge and suburban emus to Chingford, Bishops Stortford, Hertford East and Cheshunt via the Southbury Loop, and to Enfield Town. 1,123 trains daily in 1988. Fastest service to Norwich 1 hour 40 minutes (70 mph), 1938 2 hours 10 minutes (53.1 mph).

Platforms: 18.

Facilities: tickets, information, refreshments, bookstall, parcels, left luggage, taxis, LT buses nearby, Liverpool Street Underground station (Central, Metropolitan and Circle lines). Facilities at Liverpool Street are affected by the reconstruction work but will be considerably expanded as it nears completion.

Of special interest: western train shed and Great Eastern Hotel; reconstruction work.

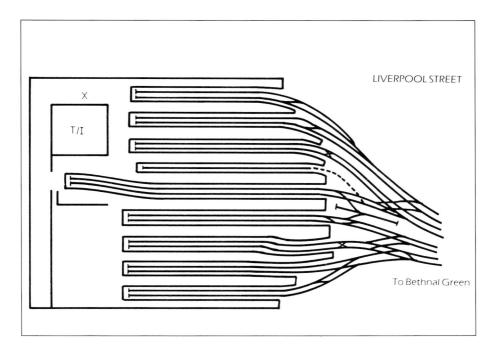

Liverpool Street, once having the worst of reputations for smoke, grime and confusion, will soon be a station transformed. Under an Act which received the Royal Assent in 1983, work began on a redevelopment scheme which embraced the closure of Broad Street station and the diversion of its trains to Liverpool Street, plus a reconstruction job there which involved rebuilding everything except the western train shed and the Great Eastern Hotel. The end product, ready in the early 1990s, will be a new Liverpool Street station with modern facilities, standard-length platforms and improved approach track and signalling. All this will be funded from the creation of 4 million sq ft of landscaped office and shop space, including public squares and other amenities. By 1988, Broad Street had been replaced by an office block, the western train shed at Liverpool Street had been renovated and a concrete raft built over the eastern one, and the rest of the station was deep in the

The western side of Liverpool Street station at the height of the reconstruction work.

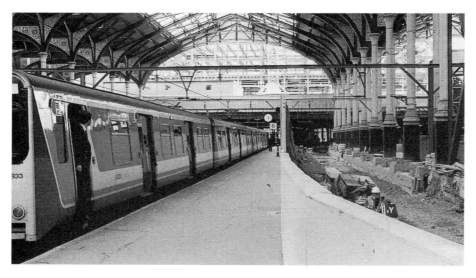

Liverpool Street kept operating while its platforms and trackwork were altered.

throes of reconstruction work.

These changes of the 1980s would have gladdened the hearts of those old Great Eastern Railway directors who voted for the original station. Its plans had been mooted to overcome the inconvenience of the old 1840 ECR terminus at Shoreditch, and it was intended to improve the railway's parlous financial position by increasing its surburban traffic receipts. There had been some thought of sharing the North London's 1865 station at Broad Street but, in a boom economy period, the Great Eastern opted for a separate station

nearby and began acquiring land in that same year. This proved much more expensive than expected and two years later the railway was in Chancery.

A new Chairman, a new General Manager and a Bill for raising £3 million in debentures started the GER recovery, and the railway was able to open a suburban station at Liverpool Street in February 1874 and the new mainline station — that beneath the western train shed — in the following November. With traffic increase expectations fulfilled, still more room became necessary resulting in the building of

Looking towards the Great Eastern Hotel with the Liverpool Street construction works on the left.

An artist's impression of the final appearance of Liverpool Street station after reconstruction is complete. (*British Rail*)

the eastern side of the station and its introduction into service in 1894. Between these opening dates, the GER commissioned C.E. and C. B. Barry to build a hotel in the space between the train shed and Liverpool Street proper, straddling the cab road. The Great Eastern Hotel was duly opened in 1884 and was refurbished in the 1899-1901 period that also added the Abercorn Rooms extension. Other railway buildings in the area included the headquarters offices at 50 Liverpool Street, the Continental Department's Harwich House, and Hamilton House further down Bishopsgate.

Electric traction, which now dominates Liverpool Street, was considered at the end of the Great Eastern era when Henry Thornton proposed a £55 million scheme to the board in 1919. Instead, a scheme of intensive steam working was chosen involving short headway sections, quick station turnrounds and controlled passenger movements. Introduced in 1920 on the Chingford, Enfield and Palace Gates lines, it became known as the 'Jazz' service from the colours used to distinguish first and third class accommodation in the high-capacity carriages. These and their ubiquitous tank locomotives shaped the travel of Liverpool Street commuters right up to 1960.

Liverpool Street got its first electric trains, to Shenfield and using 1,500 volt DC equipment, in 1949. These changed the character of the eastern side of the station (platforms 11 to 18), as the North East London electrics were later to do for the western side (platforms 1 to 8). Diesels ousted the exhilarating 'Britannia' 'Pacifics' from the long main-line platforms 9 and 10 in 1958, sharing the main line outwards with emus to Clacton and Southend.

The new Liverpool Street will doubtless be an impressive place and much better than its predecessor. Yet many will forget the shortcomings of the old station and remember its special features like the contrast between the old booking offices, the sound of Westinghouse-braked engines and the old station master's office on the long footbridge across from the badly-named Sun Street Passage to Bishopsgate. The Metropolitan Railway's trains used Liverpool Street for a few months and left traces of their route, while the rail routes out of the station still reveal remnants of the platforms below Bishopsgate goods depot and of the link to the East London line. The Gothic-style office buildings were one of the better features of Liverpool Street which the modern developers will need at least to equal.

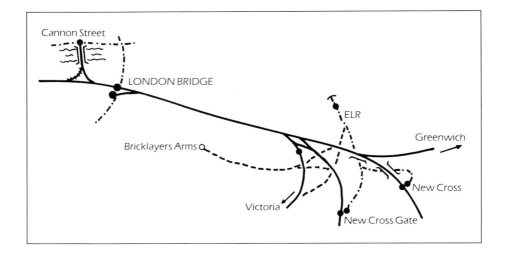

Origins: opened 1836, London & Greenwich Railway; high-level platforms opened 1864, South Eastern Railway; extensions 1866, 1879 and 1894, SER and LB&SCR. BR reconstruction completed 1978.

Location: the through platforms lie on the ex-SER Kent and South East London routes into Charing Cross and Cannon Street; the remainder of the station is the terminus for ex-LB&SCR routes from Sussex and South London. London Bridge is 76 miles from Dover Priory and 51 miles from Brighton.

Main routes: Thameslink route from the Bedford line to Gatwick Airport and Brighton; ex-LB&SCR destinations via Norwood; ex-SECR destinations via Lewisham/Greenwich; to Dover/Margate/Ramsgate, to Eastbourne/Ore, to Tunbridge Wells/Hastings and to East Grinstead.

Other routes: London Bridge to Victoria via Denmark Hill, to West Croydon, to Maidstone and 'circular' route via Crystal Palace.

Services: Thameslink services Bedford line-Gatwick/Brighton; other main-line trains to Brighton, Eastbourne (peak), Tunbridge Wells/Hastings and Tonbridge/Ashford/Sevenoaks/Dover/Margate and Ramsgate. Suburban services via Norwood to Beckenham Junction/Epsom/Peckham Rye/Caterham/Tattenham Corner/Sanderstead/West Sutton/Selhurst/Epsom Downs; also to West Croydon and East Grinstead, to Victoria via Denmark Hill and London Bridge 'circular' via Crystal Palace. Suburban emu service via Lewisham/Greenwich to Hayes/Dartford/Orpington/Gillingham/Sidcup/Barnehurst, and to Maidstone. 1,640 trains daily in 1988. Fastest service to Dover 1 hour 16 minutes (60 mph), 1938 2 hours 7 minutes (36 mph).

Platforms: 16, 10 terminal.

Facilities: ticket office and Travel Centre, refreshments, bookstall, shops, parcels and left luggage, taxis, LT bus station, London Bridge Underground station (Northern line).

Of special interest: traffic working, nineteenth and twentieth-century roofing contrasts, two station plaques.

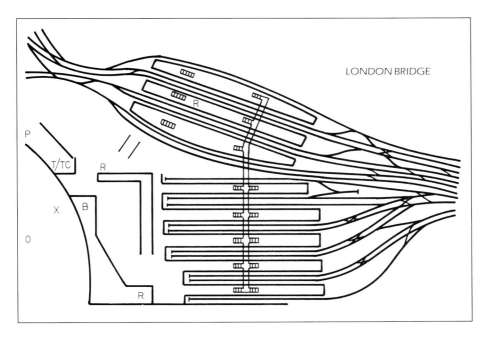

LONDON BRIDGE

Like Victoria, London Bridge originated as two stations and this is still apparent in the combination of through and terminal portions which make up the present complex. The two pre-grouping users were the South Eastern/SECR and London, Brighton & South Coast companies, the former using the high-level through platforms from which lines continue over the River Thames to Charing Cross via Waterloo East and to Cannon Street. The Southern Railway breached the boundary wall between the two former stations to create the basis for the present busy location which handles around 175,000 passengers daily.

The Lord Mayor of London attended the opening of the first station on the London Bridge site. This was on 14 December 1836 when the pioneer London & Greenwich Railway extended from Spa Road to its new two-platform London Bridge station and began operating from there to Deptford. The L&G paid £7,550 for the site which had previously been a Flemish burial ground, but the expenditure proved fully justified by the 1½ million passengers carried by the end of 1837.

The first round of development at London Bridge came on 5 June 1839 and brought in the London & Croydon Railway,

antecedent of the LB&SCR. The station was extended and made joint in 1844 when the SER and the L&G started using the north side L&C station and the latter used the expanded 1836 location along with the infant London & Brighton company. Subsequently, high tolls prompted the South Eastern to open alternative facilities at Bricklayers Arms, with the London Bridge high-level platforms then being opened in 1864 in association with the extension to Charing Cross. Further widening and remodelling took place in 1866, 1879 and 1894, with the Southern Railway then unifying the two parts of the station in 1928.

Like its contemporary London termini, London Bridge had a hotel, a seven-storey, 150-bedroom building called 'The Terminal'. After being turned into offices it was destroyed by wartime bombing, the station itself also suffering damage, especially from the incendiary attacks of 1940.

The post-war London Bridge, with many of its buildings dating back to the 1860s and scarred by the German bomber raids, was swept away in the mid-1970s as a result of a major reconstruction scheme which produced today's station. Designed by BR architects and engineers, the new London Bridge was officially opened on 15

A view of London Bridge's north side through platforms which handle the Cannon Street services.

September 1978 by the Rt Rev Mervyn Stockwood, Lord Bishop of Southwark. One of its features was a 30 ft wide covered footbridge linking the 16 platforms which had such disparate origins.

Standing between Guy's Hospital and London Bridge Hospital, the station was given a new entrance in the 1970s rebuild. This curves round from Southwark Towers towards Tooley Street and embraces a small LRT bus station plus a taxi rank. Sliding doors then lead to the station concourse with its BR travel and commercial shopping facilities. This area is covered by a modern roof based on some 115 miles of coloured steel tubing, but the country end of the terminal station still has a period three-section covering stretching from platform 9

London Bridge seen from the country end of the terminal portion and showing the long footbridge.

Despite modernization elsewhere, London Bridge retains this section of traditional overall roof.

to platform 16. Its retaining walls are in cream brick and there are iron pillars between the ridge and furrow sections and the lateral centre section. The through platforms have a modernized form of traditional buildings and canopies.

Platforms 1 to 6 accommodate London Bridge's through services, the north side dealing with the Cannon Street services and the south those to Waterloo East and Charing Cross. An Up passenger loop then precedes the first of the ex-Central platforms, No 7. From these trains run to places like Caterham and Crystal Palace and to Brighton and the Sussex coast, as well as over the Southern's first electrified route to Victoria via Denmark Hill.

The £9-million-worth of improvements at London Bridge station were preceded by a £21 million scheme of resignalling and track remodelling covering the whole area, including Charing Cross and Cannon Street. It removed the notorious Borough Market bottleneck and produced a new London Bridge signalling panel responsible for 150 miles of the most intensively used railway track in the world. The installation involves two section panels, for the South Eastern and Central divisions, some 60 ft long and handling around 250 trains an hour at busy periods. The SE panel has 257 signals and 342 sets of points, and the Central one 190 signals and 114 points.

LONDON MARYLEBONE

Origins: opened 1899, Great Central Railway. Refurbished by BR 1988-89.

Location: London terminus of ex-Great Central main line from Manchester and now of LMR Banbury and Aylesbury lines. 68¾ miles from Banbury.

Main routes: Marylebone-High Wycombe-Banbury.

Other routes: Marylebone-Aylesbury via High Wycombe and Marylebone-Aylesbury via Amersham.

Services: Marylebone-High Wycombe/Aylesbury/Banbury and Marylebone-Aylesbury. Also one Leamington Spa service. 124 trains daily in 1988. Fastest service to Aylesbury 59 minutes (37.9 mph), 1938 48 minutes (47.5 mph).

Platforms: 4.

Facilities: tickets and information, refreshments, bookstall, Marylebone LT station (Bakerloo Line), LT buses nearby.

Of special interest: main station buildings and those of former Hotel Great Central/BRB headquarters nearby; Sunday steam specials.

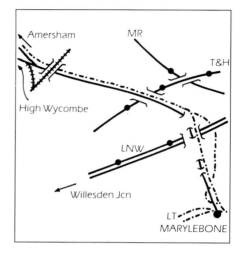

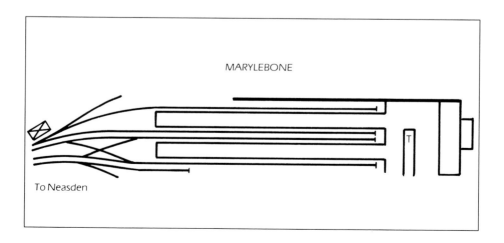

The last main-line railway into London was that of the Great Central Railway which carried coal from the middle of 1898 but could not handle passengers until Marylebone was ready for opening on 15 March the following year. By then building its new 'model' main line had so nearly exhausted the GCR's funds that its London station had to be a compromise between economy and the need to impress potential users. Hence Marylebone's impressive frontage but very ordinary interior.

By sheer enterprise the GCR built up its express and commuter business, but the route could not withstand the cost scrutinies of the 1950s and was closed north of Aylesbury from 5 September 1966. Twenty years later it seemed as if Marylebone, too, would close, and its lines pass to London Transport. Then came a 1988 BR announcement of an investment package for the Chiltern Line that would give it Networker turbo diesel trains, the latest in signalling and control, junction improvements and new information systems. As part of the package the Marylebone terminus was promised new facilities for its 9,000 daily passengers, improvements to the diesel depot located on the old steam shed site, and a carriage washing plant.

At the end of 1988 Marylebone was getting new flooring and a modern booking office in place of the stately wooden affair in the main block. This remained in its pleasant 1899 form with the

A diesel multiple unit draws into Marylebone station during December 1988.

two storeys in red brick topped by dormers and gables, with terracotta embellishments and a low tower. There is a *porte-cochère* of iron and glass and a covered way to the massive companion building on Marylebone Road. Initially the Hotel Great Central and latterly the BRB headquarters, it was the work of Robert Edis who was also involved in Liverpool Street's Great Eastern Hotel.

Marylebone uses some of its four platforms for the High Wycombe, Aylesbury and Banbury services and also deals with steam specials to Stratford-on-Avon. A two-section main roof with an east-side retaining wall covers the concourse and the ends of the platforms where the hydraulic buffers are situated.

The exuberant architecture of the station the Great Central Railway provided at Marylebone.

LONDON PADDINGTON

Origins: opened 1854, Great Western Railway, designed by Isambard Kingdom Brunel with additional features by Matthew Digby Wyatt. Concourse extension and refurbishing by BR.

Location: London terminus of WR main line from Reading and beyond. 305¼ miles from Penzance, 118½ from Bristol and 191 from Swansea.

Main routes: West of England main line to Penzance via Westbury; main lines to Bristol/Weston-super-Mare via Bath, and to South Wales via the Severn Tunnel; also Paddington-Oxford-Birmingham/Hereford, and to Cheltenham via Stroud.

Other routes: Paddington-Reading/Didcot/Oxford, and to Greenford.

Services: InterCity services to Plymouth/Penzance/Torbay via Westbury (and some via Bristol), including the 'Golden Hind Pullman', 'Cornish Riviera' and 'Night Riviera'; to Bristol/Weston-super-Mare via Bath (and Bristol Parkway), including the 'West Country Pullman' (on to Paignton); to Cardiff/Swansea/West Wales, including the 'Red Dragon Pullman', 'Saint David Executive' and 'Hibernian' (InterCity Ireland); to Oxford/Birmingham/Manchester, including the 'Stratford-upon-Avon Pullman'; and to Cheltenham/Worcester/Hereford, including the 'Cheltenham Spa Express', 'Cotswold Express' and 'Cathedrals Express'. Local services to Greenford and Reading (for Thames branches and Newbury). 318 trains daily in 1988. Fastest service to Bristol (Temple Meads) 1 hour 17 minutes (92.4 mph), 1938 1 hour 45 minutes (67.7 mph).

Platforms: 13, plus 2 used by LT trains.

Facilities: ticket office, Travel Centre, refreshments, bookstalls, fast food, shops, parcels, left luggage, parking, car hire, taxis, LT buses nearby, Paddington Underground stations (District, Metropolitan, Circle and Bakerloo lines).

Of special interest: GWR war memorial, GWR coats of arms, HQ offices oriel window and viewing balcony and GWR150 plaque on No 1 platform, Brunel statue by John Doubleday, GWR roundel and stone carvings on hotel frontage.

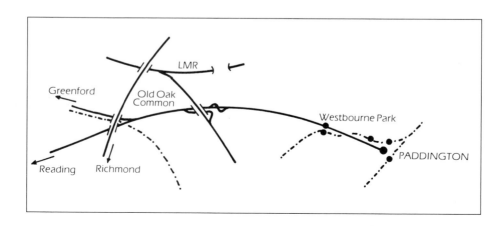

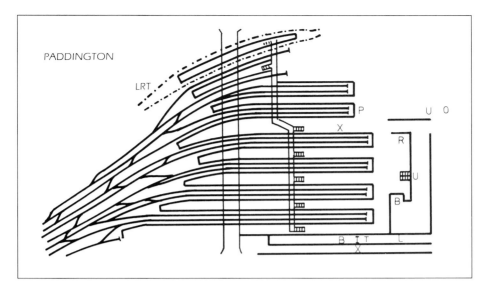

PADDINGTON

LRT

A statue of Isambard Kingdom Brunel sits in the middle of 'The Lawn' at Paddington. The great man's expression is one of quiet satisfaction, as well it might be, for although his 'broad' gauge succumbed to the 'narrow' and the early Great Western Railway trains would have seemed impossibly archaic compared with modern HSTs, yet Paddington station is still characterized by the great Brunel roof, and the Great Western Royal Hotel outside stands witness to his dream of a rail and steamer route from London to New York.

There had been indecision among the London Committee of the infant GWR over the location of its London terminus, but eventually the idea of sharing Euston was abandoned in favour of a site near the canal basin at Paddington. A temporary station, opened with the line to Maidenhead on 4 June 1838, was soon replaced by a more permanent four-platform affair, but increasing traffic soon made this inadequate too. In 1853 the decision was taken to build an entirely new station on a site between Bishops Road and Conduit Street, the departure side coming into use on 16 January 1854 and the arrival side on 29 May of that year. Each side had three

The long west-side entrance to Paddington station with the former GWR headquarters building.

A view of Paddington and its three main roof spans from below Bishops Bridge.

platform lines with five carriage lines between and a wealth of traversers and turntables to link them all together.

The main feature of the new Paddington (then called Bishops Road) was the magnificent roof, strongly influenced by the Crystal Palace and with 68 ft, 102 ft and 68 ft spans lifted on arched ribs and extending over a length of 500 ft. Brunel had worked with Matthew Digby Wyatt on the design of the station and although the hotel, completed in 1852, was the work of Philip Charles Hardwick RA, Brunel was also closely associated with the project as Chairman of the hotel company's board. The 112-bedroom hotel, acquired by the GWR in 1896, was in the style of Louis XIV with French towers rising seven storeys high.

Like most major stations, Paddington has been greatly altered over the years, its total length of platform face rising to over 10,000 ft. It had a fourth span added to the roof in 1916 and had to be repaired after extensive bomb damage in 1944. Then the end of the 1960s produced a complete remodelling which abolished the distinction between arrival and departure lines, segregated the Hammersmith & City route tracks, raised the running speeds from 10 to 25 mph, and followed the operational and

resignalling changes with a complete modernization of the passenger circulating area. The process has continued in recent years with an increase in the concourse area, the installation of the latest information systems, more shops, and now a roof renovation project.

The Paddington of the past conjures up memories of summer Saturday crowds joining the holiday trains to the West Country, journeys to connect with steamers from Weymouth or Fishguard, named trains like the 'Cornish Riviera' and the 'Cheltenham Flyer', and expresses to the Cotswolds or even the Mersey. The 'Kings', 'Castles' and 'Saints', with their attendant pannier tanks, may have gone, but Paddington remains a busy and interesting station. It has less of a suburban service than most other large London termini but handles a wealth of InterCity trains over the West of England route via Newbury, the Bristol and South Wales main line, and via Oxford to Hereford or Birmingham.

The former GWR headquarters offices (now the BRB's Macmillan House) are in Westbourne Terrace where the main cab road gives access to the station's modern ticket office and information centre above. The Lawn then extends across the ends of

One of the great roof spans at Paddington shelters an HST set and some preparations for television filming.

platforms 1 to 8 with the hotel behind. There is another cab road between platforms 8 and 9 with more BR platforms following and then numbers 15 and 16 which are used by Underground trains. Shopping and other facilities extend across the concourse and along No 1 platform from which there is a wide footbridge across to the suburban and LRT platforms.

The Underground lines are a reminder that the GWR's original 'underground' venture with the Metropolitan Railway dates back to the 1860s. The Down side milk and parcels dock and then the Up side goods shed are further reminders of past activities as the WR main line heads away west via Old Oak Common where the controlling signalling panel and the Region's London maintenance depot are located.

Part of the Paddington concourse, with Brunel surveying his handiwork.

TO TRAINS

LONDON ST PANCRAS

Origins: opened 1868, Midland Railway, engineer W. R. Barlow; hotel added 1873, architect Sir Gilbert Scott.

Location: North London terminus of former Midland main line, 167 miles from Sheffield.

Main routes: London to Nottingham/Sheffield via Derby.

Other routes: London-Bedford.

Services: InterCity services to Nottingham, Derby/Sheffield and Leeds, including the 'Master Cutler'. Early and late local electric trains plus peak fast service to Bedford. 74 trains daily in 1988. Fastest service to Sheffield 2 hours 18 minutes (72.6 mph), 1938 3 hours 2 minutes (55.1 mph).

Platforms: 6.

Facilities: ticket office, Travel Centre, refreshments, bookstall, parcels, left luggage, car hire, taxis, parking, King's Cross & St Pancras Underground station (Metropolitan, Circle, Victoria and Piccadilly lines), LT buses pass nearby.

Of special interest: former Midland Grand Hotel, single-span station roof with ironwork by the Butterley Company, Derbyshire, 1867, traditional booking hall and panelled ticket office, Somers Town goods depot site.

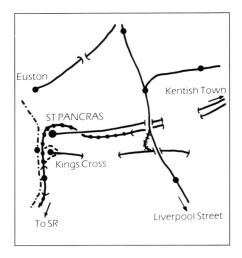

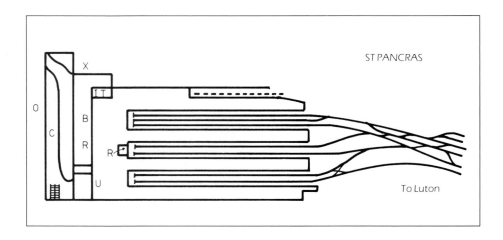

The exit from St Pancras, now embraced in a major redevelopment scheme for the whole area.

The Midland Railway had its headquarters at Derby and its initial access to London was via Bedford to Hitchin and then over Great Northern metals into King's Cross. Since the two railways were rivals in many areas it is hardly surprising that these arrangements were unsatisfactory, leading the Midland to build a separate route to London and create there one of the most striking of stations. In doing so there is little doubt that the MR went out of its way to put Euston and King's Cross in the shade.

First came the train shed, opened in 1868 and raised above street level to avoid the gradients suffered by its neighbours. Using Butterley's Derbyshire ironwork, engineer W. H. Barlow gave the station a great single-span roof, 240 ft wide and 100 ft high, with decorated side walls and with a panelled booking office on the west side. The ground floor was designed specially for the storage of Burton beer with access by wagon hoist. But all this was rather eclipsed by the opening of 'The Midland Grand Hotel' in 1873. Gilbert Scott won the MR design competition and produced a dramatic Gothic structure with interior decoration to match.

St Pancras station has lost its Scottish traffic, the Heysham and Tilbury boat trains, and the GER services to Cambridge, but it remains busy with trains to Sheffield and the East Midlands. The tunnel route beneath its Churchyard carriage sidings and the old Somers Town goods depot also carries Thameslink services from the Bedford line to the SR. Ahead, there are plans to link St Pancras and King's Cross in a massive development scheme including offices, housing, leisure and other community facilities.

From the entrance to the former hotel, a rising roadway runs along its five-storey frontage which is topped by an array of towers, pinnacles, chimneys and other embellishments. An arch leads motor vehicles to the west-side station entrance and the traditional booking hall and ticket office, a further vehicle roadway running between platforms 5 and 6. The great curved roof covers the concourse and a large area of the surviving six platforms.

An HST set and a fair amount of Royal Mail paraphernalia beneath the great overall roof of St Pancras.

LONDON VICTORIA

Origins: Central side originally opened 1860, Chatham side 1862. Former rebuilt 1908, London, Brighton & South Coast Railway, architect Sir Charles Morgan; latter rebuilt 1909, South Eastern & Chatham Railway, A. W. Blomfield. BR remodelling and commercial development above west side.

Location: London West End terminus of ex-SECR routes from the Medway, North Kent and Dover, and of ex-LB&SCR routes from East and West Sussex via the Brighton main line. 77¼ miles from Dover, 51 from Brighton.

Main routes: Chatham main line to Dover and Ramsgate via Faversham, and Brighton main line to Horsham, Haywards Heath, Brighton and Littlehampton/Bognor Regis/Portsmouth; also Eastbourne/Hastings via Lewes. Gatwick Express to Gatwick Airport.

Other routes: Surrey routes (West Sutton, West Croydon, etc); Oxted and East Grinstead; mid-Kent routes (Sevenoaks, Ashford, etc); Victoria-London Bridge.

Services: patterned electric services to Dover and Ramsgate via Faversham; to Bromley South, Swanley, Ashford and Sevenoaks; to Horsham, Haywards Heath, Brighton and west to Littlehampton/Bognor Regis/Portsmouth Harbour; to Lewes (for Seaford) and Eastbourne/Hastings; to Oxted (for Uckfield) and East Grinstead. Local emu services to West Sutton, West Croydon, Horsham, Tattenham Corner, Crystal Palace, Sanderstead and London Bridge. Special Gatwick Express service non-stop to Gatwick Airport and additional peak period services, eg to Gillingham/Rochester, Burgess Hill/West Worthing, Selhurst/

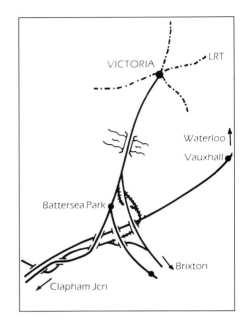

Beckenham Junction. 1,220 trains daily in 1988. Fastest service to Dover 1 hour 40 minutes (46.3 mph) and to Brighton 51 minutes (60 mph); 1938 2 hours 15 minutes (34.3 mph) and 1 hour (51 mph) respectively.

Platforms: 17.

Facilities: tickets, information, refreshments, bookstalls, parcels, left luggage, car hire, taxis, Victoria Underground station (Circle, District and Victoria lines), LT buses outside and coach stations nearby, Tourist Information Centre, LT information, European Rail Travel Centre, Victoria Place shopping complex.

Of special interest: dual station frontage, decorated roof support pillars, LB&SCR war memorial, Continental and Gatwick Express facilities, Victoria Place shopping development.

Victoria is a large, fascinating and cosmopolitan station which originated as the West End terminus of two major railway systems and now deals with over 200,000 passengers on the busiest days. In addition to its extensive commuter business it serves large numbers of travellers to and from the Channel Ports and many others using the special train service which links the London terminal with Gatwick Airport. Victoria is quite near Buckingham Palace and is the Southern Region's 'royal' terminal, where the Queen welcomes visiting Heads of State or joins the Royal Train on Derby Day.

Opened as two separate stations, Victoria remained that way for over 60 years until a hole was knocked in the wall between them in 1924. Its two sections are still apparent, platforms 1 to 8 making up the 'Chatham' side and providing services to the Medway towns and the Kent coast, and the remainder constituting the 'Central' part of the station which provides services along the main line to Brighton and the rest of Sussex. The Chatham side commemorates the former London, Chatham & Dover Railway and the later South Eastern & Chatham, while Central refers to the Southern Railway's Central Division, inherited from the London, Brighton & South Coast Railway.

The original Victoria station development was the work of the Victoria Station & Pimlico Railway, a terminal company formed to extend the main line railway access to London across the Thames. The LC&DR and LB&SCR were shareholders in the smaller company although the 'Brighton' eventually opted for a separate station within the Victoria site and, as the senior partner, got its facilities first. The LB&SCR station, with ten tracks and access via Eccleston Bridge and Victoria Street, was opened on 1 October 1860. It was then used by LC&DR trains from 3 December until that company's own nine-track station was ready for use from 25 August 1862. The latter had its entrance in Wilton Road and included some mixed gauge track to permit its use by GWR services from Southall.

The original double station at Victoria was not a very attractive affair and moves to effect an improvement were made by both companies around the turn of the century. Again the Brighton produced results first, Sir Charles Morgan giving the west side a new frontage and roof in the style of the times and matching the

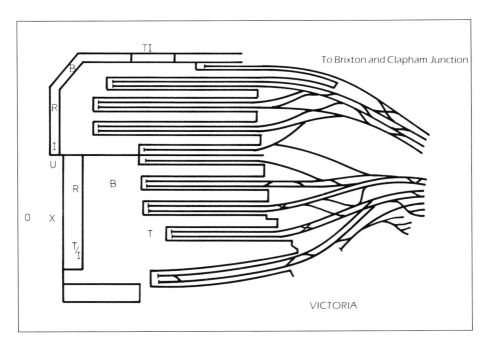

TI

To Brixton and Clapham Junction

VICTORIA

The busy approaches to Victoria with the Grosvenor Hotel on the right and the 'Chatham' side on the left.

A VSOE train stands in Victoria station with the outline of the huge commercial developments beyond.

300-bedroom Grosvenor Hotel which also dated from the 1860-61 period. The SECR, a combination of the South Eastern and Chatham systems, completed its rebuilding work in 1909, a year after its neighbour. A. W. Blomfield designed the SECR frontage which was executed in Portland stone and, whilst matching the LB&SCR design, was sufficiently different to make the separate ownership obvious. This separation, which included a duplication of all facilities from the two station-masters downwards, was to continue until control passed to the Southern Railway with the 1923 grouping.

The development of facilities at Victoria has continued over the years, the present decade producing an extra two platforms for the use of airport trains plus a raft over platforms 9 to 17 to accommodate an office block and the rail-air terminal. Following these changes came the complete resignalling of 267 miles of track in and beyond the station and the concentration of movement control on a Victoria Signalling Centre at Clapham Junction.

The Chatham side of Victoria station has offices along Wilton Road including the European Rail Travel Centre behind the long 1/2 platforms. Two arched roof spans then cover the concourse end of the station which has further specialist accommodation on Platform 8 for dealing with Continental arrivals and including Venice Simplon Orient Express and Hover-speed buildings. The shuttle service to the new 'Battersea' leisure complex will use Platform 1.

The Central side of the station has its platforms set further back, behind a large circulating area where a wealth of facilities are provided beneath the ridge and furrow roof section. Beyond this the platforms themselves lie beneath a modern commercial development which includes the Victoria Place shopping complex. Platforms 14 and 15 are used by the Gatwick Express trains and have their own ticket office, this innovation contrasting with the older buildings adjoining the station-side entrance to the Grosvenor Hotel.

There is an LB&SCR war memorial near the hotel-side station entrance. Victoria also has Underground access here and near the Chatham frontage, and LT buses operate from the depot in front of the station. There are also two coach stations, one in Buckingham Palace Road and the other in Wilton Road.

LONDON WATERLOO

Origins: main station opened 1922 on 1848 site, London & South Western Railway, architect James Robb Scott. Waterloo East opened 1869, Waterloo & City line 1898.

Location: south bank London terminus of former LSWR main line. 79¼ miles from Southampton, 143 from Weymouth.

Main routes: Waterloo-Weymouth main line, also to Portsmouth via Guildford and Exeter via Salisbury; plus Waterloo East routes as for Charing Cross.

Other routes: 'Windsor' lines to Windsor, Kingston-on-Thames and Reading; to Brookwood/Alton, Woking and Guildford; to Guildford, Shepperton, Chessington, Hampton Court, Dorking and Surbiton. Also Waterloo East routes as for Charing Cross. Waterloo & City underground line to Bank.

Services: main-line services, including Wessex Electrics, to Basingstoke, Southampton, Wareham and Weymouth, including the 'Royal Wessex'; also main-line electrics to Portsmouth Harbour via Guildford and loco-motive-hauled services to Salisbury and Exeter. 'Windsor' line services to Windsor & Eton Riverside, Kingston-on-Thames, Reading and Waterloo (Circular). Emus to Brookwood/Alton, Woking and Guildford; also to Guildford (via Effingham Junction), Shepperton, Hampton Court, Dork-ing and Surbiton. From Waterloo East services to Kent resorts via Ashford, to Hastings, and on South East London routes out to Orpington, Dartford and Gravesend. Intensive service on Waterloo & City underground line. Main station 1,369 trains daily in 1988 plus 779 at Waterloo East and 338 on Waterloo & City line. Fastest service to Weymouth 2 hours 23 minutes (61.3 mph), 1938 2 hours 54 minutes (49.3 mph).

Platforms: 21.

Facilities: tickets, Travel Centre, re-freshments, bookstalls, shops, parcels, left luggage, parking, car hire, taxis, Red Arrow bus service 307, LT buses nearby, Waterloo Underground sta-tion (Northern and Bakerloo lines).

Of special interest: Victory Arch war memorial, period notices, turret clock, Ransome & Rapier buffer sets, and Waterloo & City Line.

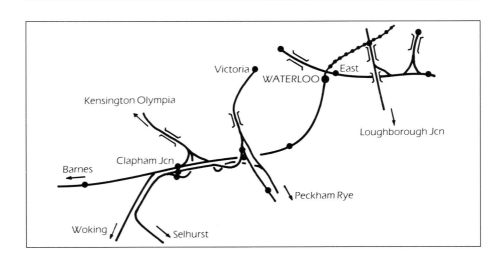

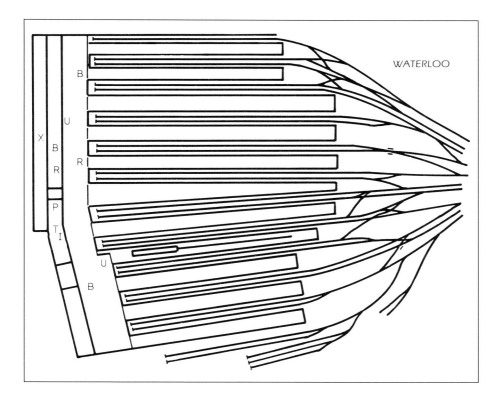

WATERLOO

Waterloo is British Rail's largest station, covering an area of 24½ acres and dealing with nearly a quarter of a million passengers a day. Its rail routes vary from the unremarkable suburban ones to the prestige operation of the Wessex Electrics on the Weymouth main line. Externally the station presents an imposing traditional appearance but inside it houses many modern features, presenting passengers with clear and plentiful train information and offering a wide range of goods and services. The main station has a satellite in Waterloo East which links it to London Bridge and stations to the east, and it has its own underground connection to the City of London in the shape of the Waterloo & City line.

The story of Waterloo starts on 11 July 1848 when the London & South Western Railway opened the first station on the site. It took over from a terminal which the pioneer London & Southampton Railway had opened at Nine Elms, that location subsequently becoming important in its own right for locomotive and freight

activity. At Waterloo, the new four-platform station was a modest affair, built with an eye on extending to London Bridge and taking up the area now occupied by platforms 7 to 11. As so often happened at that period, it soon proved inadequate and was replaced in 1853.

The 1853 Waterloo station was itself extended a number of times. An almost immediate, and unusual, addition was that of the 'Cemetery Station' of the Necropolis & National Mausoleum Company which ran a regular service of trains for coffins and mourners to a cemetery at Brookwood. In 1860 what became known as the 'Windsor Station' was added to Waterloo. This was a semi-separate operation now represented by platforms 16 to 21 which still have their own distinctive roof to denote their original separate identity. The plan to extend to London Bridge was implemented in the form of an awkward single line across the main station concourse, and other extensions were made in 1878 and 1885 resulting in a very muddled, piecemeal bit of railway.

The exit from Waterloo as seen from the 'Windsor Station'.

At the end of the century the London & South Western was forced to commit itself to rebuilding Waterloo, a process that proved as piecemeal as its growth. The first stage was a new set of platforms 1 to 5, with further major alterations in 1911-19 and completion in time for commissioning on 21 March 1922, just before the Southern Railway took over. The rebuilt station was given a new frontage, a curved block in the style of the day and the work of the LSWR's chief architectural assistant, James Robb Scott. One of its most notable features is the elaborate Victory Arch in Portland stone, reminding the thousands who pass through it daily of the LSWR railwaymen who gave their lives in the First World War, and of the 626 SR men who died in the Second. Other notable features of the new station were the main booking hall and the Surrey Dining Rooms.

Inside the station, the two-acre concourse and its Travel Centre and other facilities are followed by the 21 platforms, the lower numbers used by inner suburban services, followed by the trains to Woking and Guildford, the main-line services and

then the complex of cab road and arrival lines. The 1920 administrative block known as 'The Village' separates these platforms from those used by the Windsor and Reading line trains. All the platform lines then come together as eight Up and Down Suburban, Through and Windsor tracks, controlled from the signal box and station operations centre above platforms 7 and 8.

Opened as Waterloo Junction on 1 January 1869, Waterloo East consists of a centre island and two outer platforms to serve the paired fast and slow lines linking Charing Cross and the approaches to London Bridge. It is reached by footbridge from the opposite side of the Waterloo road approaches. The third Waterloo station lies below the others, with lift access for its rolling stock. It is the two-platform terminus of the Waterloo & City line, known affectionately as 'The Drain'. The Waterloo & City was conceived by the LSWR to give it access to the City of London and it still performs this function. Opened on 8 August 1898, the 1 mile 12 yard route runs in 12 ft 1¾ in diameter

A view of Waterloo giving some impression of the sheer size of the station.

tunnels and uses multiple unit trains operating at a 4-minute interval in the peak.

Important for its traffic levels and as the SR headquarters, Waterloo will gain a terminal for the 1993 Channel Tunnel traffic and is already the subject of a major resignalling scheme based on a new signalling centre at Wimbledon.

MANCHESTER VICTORIA PICCADILLY

LYR/LMS/LMR
BR/LMR

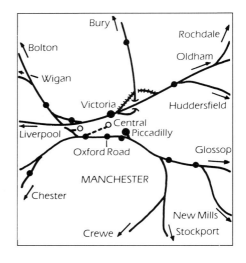

Origins: Victoria station originated in 1844, with a major rebuild in 1881-84, enlargement in 1904, and a new frontage in 1909; Lancashire & Yorkshire Railway, William Dawes. Oxford Road station originated in 1849 and Piccadilly in 1960 when it took over from the 1842 London Road site.

Location: Victoria links the Bury and cross-Pennine lines with the routes to Blackburn, Wigan, Liverpool and Preston. Piccadilly has Crewe, Stoke, Sheffield, Buxton and Glossop lines terminating and routes out via Oxford Road to Chester and Liverpool. Piccadilly is 188¼ miles from Euston.

Main routes: Piccadilly — to South, South West and South Wales, to Euston via Stafford, and Blackpool/Liverpool-Manchester-Sheffield-East Anglia. Victoria — to Preston/Blackpool, Cumbria and Scotland, from Liverpool to Scarborough/York/Newcastle via Leeds and from North Wales to Hull.

Local routes: Piccadilly to Stoke/Stafford/Birmingham, to Hadfield, to New Mills Central, and to Crewe/Alderley, Altrincham and Liverpool via Oxford Road. The latter also has routes to Hunts Bank and Chester. Victoria to Leeds, Shaw/Rochdale, to Wigan and Kirkby/Southport, to Bolton and Blackburn, and to Earlestown/Liverpool.

Services: InterCity services from Piccadilly to Euston, including the 'Manchester Express', 'Manchester Pullman' and sleepers; also to Brighton, Poole and South West via Birmingham and to South Wales via Shrewsbury. Sprinters link Liverpool/Blackpool with East Anglia via Oxford Road and Piccadilly, including the 'Loreley', Piccadilly also having hourly fast trains to Sheffield, and the former to Chester. Victoria originates services to the northern West Coast Main Line

destinations via Preston and has cross-country services from Chester/North Wales to Hull and Liverpool to Leeds/York/Scarborough/Newcastle. Middle-distance services run from Victoria to Kirkby/Southport, Blackpool, Leeds and Liverpool, and from Piccadilly to Birmingham/Stafford, while there are local routes to Alderley/Crewe, Earlestown, Wigan, Shaw/Rochdale, Hadfield, New Mills Central, Altrincham and Buxton. Piccadilly had 811 trains daily in 1988, Victoria 679 and Oxford Road 319. Fastest service to London 2 hours 25 minutes (77.9 mph), 1938 3 hours 15 minutes (57.9 mph).

Platforms: Piccadilly — 13; Victoria — 12, including 6 bays; Oxford Road — 5, including one bay.

Facilities: ticket, information, refreshments, bookstall, parcels, left luggage, car hire and taxi facilities at both main stations, parking adjacent to both and special bus stops including airport service from Victoria. Buses from Piccadilly approach road, and bus station nearby. Tickets, refreshments, some parking, taxi rank and local buses at Oxford Road.

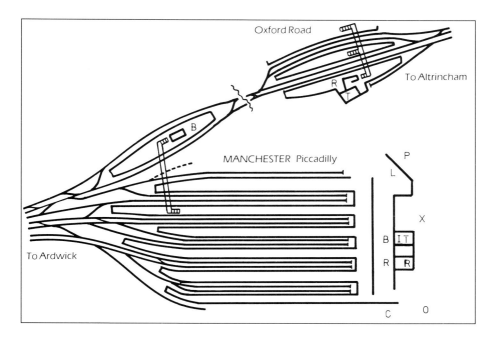

MANCHESTER Piccadilly

Manchester has two great stations, Victoria, which stands by the rivers Irk and Irwell north of the city centre, and Piccadilly, on London Road just beyond the Rochdale Canal. Victoria is a traditional station brought up to date and handling both through and terminating services. It is especially important for movements from Lancashire and the coast to the Yorkshire side of the Pennines. Piccadilly's terminal

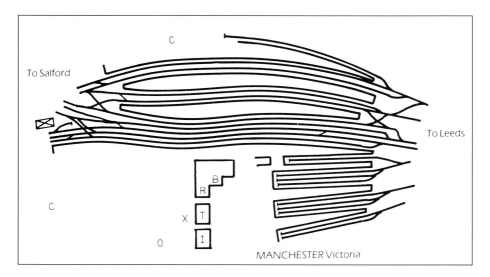

MANCHESTER Victoria

87 030 stands on a Euston train at Manchester Piccadilly.

platforms handle the InterCity services from London and the south, and its elevated through platforms deal with cross-country links such as those from East Anglia to Liverpool and Blackpool. These also call at Oxford Road, Manchester's other central station. All these locations have a substantial volume of local and commuter business.

The early railways of Manchester were generally elevated routes, cohabiting with waterway traffic sites rather than pushing on into the city centre. Its first line was, of course, that of the Liverpool & Manchester, ceremonially opened to Liverpool Road station on 15 September 1830. Although later relegated to goods depot status, the

A view of the corner of the main building at Manchester Victoria.

'Rocket 150' celebrations of the L&M anniversary prompted the revival of the location as part of a major museum project.

The Grand Junction Railway linked Manchester with the south from 1837, the Bolton line reaching Salford in 1838 and the Manchester & Birmingham opening to Stockport in 1840, its temporary Manchester terminus being replaced by a new one at London Road from 8 May 1842. This took in the Sheffield trains and was then linked with the Altrincham line seven years later. The London Road station was rebuilt and enlarged in 1866 and subsequently absorbed the Midland Railway's services. It lasted then until the West Coast electrification demanded remodelling to accommodate the 25kV services from which it emerged as the present Piccadilly in September 1960. Oxford Road, which originated in 1849 as the terminus of the MSJ&A line from Altrincham, was rebuilt at that time.

Victoria station dates from 1 January 1844 when the link from Miles Platting was opened and then extended to Ordsall Lane. Initially a single long platform with some hair-raising working arrangements, it became steadily more inadequate until 1884 brought a major enlargement. In the same year the LNWR opened its own Exchange station on the other side of the river because the LYR would not agree to joint ownership of Victoria. The latter was further enlarged in 1904 and received a new frontage block in 1909, but Exchange has been closed.

The through platform north side of Manchester Victoria station.

The Cheshire Lines Committee obtained access to Manchester from 9 July 1877, using a temporary terminus which was then replaced by Central station three years later. The through services from King's Cross and St Pancras used Central, and the Midland Hotel was built opposite in 1898. The station closed on 5 May 1969 when a new junction at Cornbrook allowed its remaining trains to be handled by Piccadilly, but it was subsequently restored to use as an exhibition centre.

The substantial four-storey main station building at Victoria still proclaims its ancestry with 'Lancashire & Yorkshire Railway' and 'Victoria Station' lettered into the frontage and corner tower, and with a huge LYR map above the war memorials on the concourse. The older section of the external canopy still has the principal LYR destinations picked out in coloured glass, the roof supports bear the legend 'Ardwick Ironworks 1864' and the marbled refreshment room retains an atmosphere of period splendour. To match all this the ticket office modernization has been in wood to a traditional design. Beyond the concourse facilities are the bays of the terminal section of the station, then the long No 11 platform with a 31½ milepost near West Junction signal box, and subway access to five more through platforms.

At Piccadilly a rising approach road leads to the plain modern frontage in brick and wood, and to the adjacent ten-storey block and parcels office. An arcade leads to the main concourse where 11 platforms are covered by two main arches with two more staggered spans on the London Road side, all supported on massive iron columns and with a multi-colour brick retaining wall. No 11 platform line is now used for parcels, No 12 has been lifted and Nos 13 and 14 pass around the elevated island of the through portion of the station. Piccadilly has recently benefited from a £9 million track and signalling modernization programme which has connected it with the May 1988 Windsor Link line.

Piccadilly's through services continue to Oxford Road where the two running lines become four platform lines through the two islands and single Down platform. The Up side island has a line for originating and terminating services at its outer face and also houses the administration block which includes the ticket office and a buffet. The frontage lies at an angle from the through lines and has an outward-curved facade in wood and in the same style as the platform canopy supports.

As this book was about to go to press, the Minister of State for Transport announced the go-ahead for the Manchester Metrolink Light Railway. The first new, street-running light railway to be authorized in this country for years, the 'supertram' system, which should be operational by 1992, will provide a link between BR's Piccadilly and Victoria stations. The rapid transit scheme also provides for the take-over and conversion of BR lines from Bury and Altrincham.

MARGATE

Origins: opened 1926 by Southern Railway on site of 1863 London, Chatham & Dover Railway station.

Location: on ex-London, Chatham & Dover Railway (later SECR) route from Victoria to Ramsgate via Faversham. 78 miles from Charing Cross via Canterbury West, 73¾ miles from Victoria.

Main routes: to Charing Cross via Ramsgate and Canterbury West, and to Victoria via Faversham.

Other routes: local service to and from Ramsgate with links to Dover via Deal.

Services: main-line electric services Margate-Charing Cross via Canterbury West and Ashford, and Ramsgate-Margate-Victoria via Faversham. Some services to Cannon Street and London Bridge. Local Ramsgate service provided by the longer-distance trains, and links from there to Dover via Deal. 114 trains daily in 1988. Fastest service to London 1 hour 37 minutes (45.6 mph), 1938 1 hour 23 minutes (53.3 mph).

Platforms: 4.

Facilities: tickets, Travel Centre, refreshments, bookstall, parcels and left luggage, parking, taxis, local buses

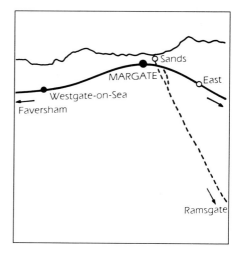

nearby.

Of special interest: main station building, including external decoration and booking hall clock, Down platform water tank, new Networker train mural in station subway.

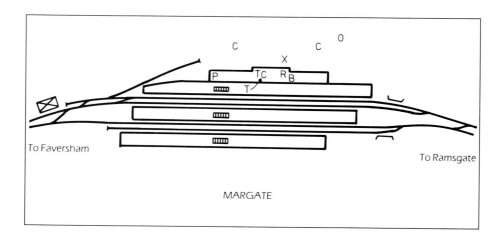

MARGATE

The style of the 1926 station at Margate was to become a feature of the newly-formed Southern Railway.

Margate is a busy holiday resort in summer with a long sandy front and plenty of entertainment for the thousands of day-trippers who come from the London and Medway areas. Rail passenger journeys are 150 per cent higher than in the winter months when the sizeable Margate station seems a bit awe-inspiring for its comparatively modest task. Even so, it has an excellent service of originating and terminating Charing Cross trains over the ex-SER route plus calls by the Ramsgate trains on the former LC&DR route to Victoria.

Its former carriage cleaning work having been transferred elsewhere, the track layout at Margate has been simplified with the loss of the Up bay and sidings. The complex now consists of the main platform served by the Down main, an island served by the Down platform loop and Up main, and an Up platform where the former loop has been altered to a dead end. The principal buildings are on the Down, seaward side and consist of an entrance hall and wings, but larger and more ornate than those at Ramsgate. The brick frontage has polished stone facings with roundels depicting transport themes. There is an

ornate clock housing inside the ticket hall, a water tank structure at one end of the Down platform and a former parcels dock at the other. Further west stands the tall signal box which controls the station workings.

Margate got its first trains on 1 December 1846 when the SER line from Ashford reached a terminus called Margate Sands. Its second railway dates from 5 October 1863 when the LC&DR-backed Kent Coast line reached the present site, then known as Margate West. It had been intended to continue from the latter, but the two routes were linked instead. Soon after its formation the Southern Railway obtained a Ministry of Transport Order permitting the rationalization of the whole Thanet area. The implementation of this, from 2 July 1926, closed the SER route from Ramsgate to the Margate Sands terminus in favour of the ex-LC&DR line along the coast, and concentrated all traffic on a new station — the present one — on the Margate West site. There was a smaller station at Ramsgate East opened in 1870, but this closed in 1953.

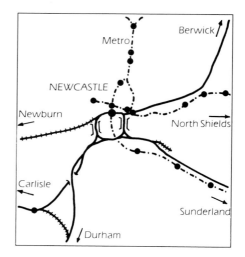

Origins: built 1849-50, Newcastle & Berwick Railway, architect John Dobson; portico added 1860 and 1893 extension, North Eastern Railway; new BR Travel Centre 1985.

Location: East Coast Main Line, junction with Sunderland and Carlisle lines. 268¾ miles from King's Cross.

Main routes: King's Cross-Newcastle/Scotland; North East-South Wales/South West/South Coast via Birmingham; Newcastle-Liverpool and Newcastle-Carlisle.

Other routes: Sunderland-Newcastle-Hexham; Newcastle-Morpeth/Alnmouth/Berwick; Newcastle-Sunderland/Middlesbrough.

Services: InterCity services on the East Coast Main Line to King's Cross and to Scotland, including the 'Flying Scotsman', 'Highland Chieftain', 'Aberdonian', 'Talisman', 'Cleveland Executive' and 'Tees-Tyne Pullman'; and on the North East-South West route via Birmingham to Cardiff, Penzance and Poole and including the 'Devonian', 'Cornishman' and 'Northumbrian'. Liverpool services via Leeds and Manchester. Semi-fasts to Carlisle and local services Hexham-Newcastle-Sunderland; also to Middlesbrough and to Morpeth/Alnmouth/Berwick-on-Tweed. 291 trains daily in 1988. Fastest service to London 3 hours (89.6 mph), 1938 4 hours (67.2 mph).

Platforms: 9, including 6 bays.

Facilities: tickets and Travel Centre, refreshments, bookstall, parcels, left luggage, car hire, parking, taxis, local buses, Metro interchange station.

Of special interest: station frontage and hotel, Tyne bridges, Metro systems, museums at Middle Engine Lane, and at Monkwearmouth and Wylam.

An adjunct to the electrification of the East Coast Main Line is the remodelling of the complex track layout at Newcastle. This will effect the notable diamond crossovers at Newcastle East but will not reduce the interest of this major railway location where the long, imposing frontage of the nineteenth century provides a striking contrast with the colourful steel and armoured glass construction of the Travel Centre opened by the Duke of Edinburgh on 5 December 1985.

The lower reaches of the Tyne were served by early wagonways carrying coal from local pits to coasting vessels, and it was fitting that the area should feature prominently in the early years of the conventional railway age. George Stephenson came from nearby Wylam, a village close to the route of the pioneer Newcastle & Carlisle Railway which opened its first section of line, between Blaydon and Hexham, in 1835 and then edged nearer to Newcastle proper along both banks of the Tyne. Four years later a line was opened between North Shields and Manors, followed quickly by the Brandling Junction Railway's route from Monkwearmouth and South Shields to Gateshead and a connection to the N&C there.

By the late 1840s Newcastle had railways east and west along both banks of the Tyne. The elements of a north-south trunk route existed and the time had clearly come for a great joining up process and a single central station. The first work to be completed was the High Level Bridge, passing 100 ft above the River Tyne and completing the rail route from London to Berwick. This double-deck structure was the work of Robert Stephenson and the opening of the permanent bridge in 1849 was followed by John Dobson's Central station in 1850, a link to the Scotswood line in 1851 and the Royal Station Hotel in 1854. The opening of the Royal Border Bridge at Berwick in 1850 had not only kept Queen Victoria busy with opening ceremonies but had completed the rail link from Newcastle to Edinburgh.

The newly formed North Eastern Railway elected for an administrative centre at York so the Newcastle & Berwick Railway's original plans for Newcastle station were only partly implemented, the portico not being added until Thomas Prosser's era. William Bell added to the roof spans in 1893, the number of platforms was increased, and then the addition of the King Edward Bridge in 1906 created the present 'box' configuration of lines and a considerable increase in operational flexibility. The NER introduced electrification on the lines north of the Tyne to win back traffic from the tramways, and the latest changes at Newcastle have also been linked with that form of traction. First came tunnels to carry the new Metro rapid transit system trains beneath Central station, and now it is the scene of track remodelling and the erection of overhead equipment for the ECML electrification.

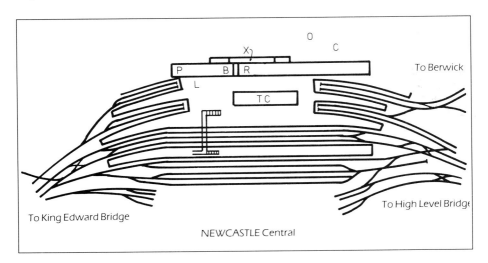

NEWCASTLE Central

A variety of multiple units in the east-end bays at Newcastle station.

The first naming of an InterCity 125 HST power car at Newcastle Central station on 26 April 1983. (*British Rail*)

Access to Newcastle station is through the great 1860 portico, leading to a spacious concourse lying between the east and west end bays. The main roof span then covers the three tracks between platforms 8 and 9, the latter forming an island with platform 10 and lines W, X, Y and Z lying beyond but still within the third curved roof span. Additional lines then run outside the retaining wall. The station's main facilities are housed on the concourse and include the futuristic-looking Travel Centre.

Central station concourse also gives access to the Metro urban transport network. This electrified railway rapid transit system was authorized by an Act of 1973 and opened in sections between 1980 and 1984. It took over the routes electrified by the NER in 1904 and the LNER in 1934 to provide services over a route from Bank Foot to South Shields and on the coastal loop out through Tynemouth and Whitley Bay. Four route permutations provide coverage of the Metro network using double cars operating in pairs and controlled from a signalling centre at South Gosforth. The modern stations provide interchange with BR, local bus services and with the ferry operating across the Tyne between North and South Shields.

In addition to the complexities of the Newcastle station area, including its assortment of Tyne bridges, the Metro routes to South Shields and to Tynemouth are also of high interest, as is the BR line to Carlisle which follows the course of the Tyne and has some very attractive station buildings. There are more on the ECML north to Berwick and the area is rich in rail museums — at Beamish, Monkwearmouth, Wylam and Middle Engine Lane.

Newcastle station is an interchange point between the ECML, North East/South West and Liverpool routes and more local services to Hexham, Berwick and Middlesbrough via Sunderland. Trains to Glasgow and Stranraer via Carlisle have recently added to the station activity.

The main concourse at Newcastle with the modern Travel Centre structure on the right.

NORWICH THORPE

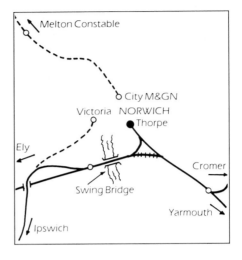

Origins: opened 1886, Great Eastern Railway, architects John Wilson and W. N. Ashbee. BR remodelling 1987.

Location: terminus for lines from Liverpool Street, Ely and Norfolk Coast. 115 miles from Liverpool Street.

Main routes: Liverpool Street via Ipswich and Birmingham/Liverpool/Cambridge via Ely.

Other routes: to Ely, Sheringham, Yarmouth and Lowestoft.

Services: electric InterCity services via Ipswich to Liverpool Street, including the 'East Anglian'. Sprinters to Cambridge via Ely, and to Birmingham/Liverpool via Ely and Peterborough. Local trains to Yarmouth/Lowestoft, to Cromer and Sheringham and on Ely line. 190 trains daily in 1988. Fastest service to London 1 hour 40 minutes (69 mph), 1938 2 hours 10 minutes (53.1 mph).

Platforms: 6.

Facilities: ticket office/Travel Centre, refreshments, bookstall, parcels, left luggage, car hire, parking, taxis, Eastern Counties buses.

Of special interest: 1886 main station buildings, 1921 goods depot offices, pre-alteration destination board on platform 6, Crown Point depot, Wensum swing bridge, flint building at Trowse.

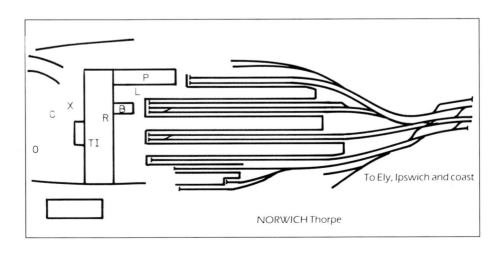

NORWICH Thorpe

The imposing station frontage at Norwich, once accommodating the District Officer's staff.

Norwich used to have four passenger stations: Victoria, terminus of the 1849 Eastern Union Railway; City, which the Eastern & Midlands opened in 1882; Trowse, near the junction of the Ipswich and Cambridge routes; and the surviving Norwich Thorpe. The latter took over Victoria's trains in 1916, the Trowse passengers in 1939, and has outlived the M&GN City station which had been demolished in the heavy bombing of Norwich in 1942 but did stay open until 1959 when the old M&GN system was virtually abolished.

Norfolk's first railway was the Norwich & Yarmouth which opened from the coast to Norwich on 1 May 1844 with a combined station and headquarters on what was later the goods depot site. The Norwich & Brandon Railway reached Trowse on 30 July 1845 and was linked with the N&Y later that year via a crossing of the River Wensum, now spanned by a swing bridge unique in carrying the 25kV wires of the electrified route from London to Norwich.

The surviving station at Norwich lies in a bend of the Wensum, not far from the city centre. It has an impressive frontage designed by the Great Eastern architect John Wilson and brought into use in 1886. The main two-storey block has a porte-cochère with parapet above and then an elaborate clock pediment fronting a pavilion roof. The warm red brick construction is extensively supplemented by stone-work which is especially varied around the window openings and access archways.

The latter lead to the booking hall with its pleasantly decorated ceiling and to the main concourse where a six-section roof covers part of the platform area as well.

The 1987 electrification to Norwich was accompanied by an extension of the station concourse and a remodelling of the approaches to the six platforms, still busy with London, coast and cross-country trains even if the Dereham, Swaffham, Wells and Coltishall workings have gone. The area's maintenance depot is in a new location alongside the link between the London and Yarmouth lines, with the old flint buildings of Trowse lying a little way along the former. Norwich loco shed is no more, but the adjacent goods depot retains both work and its 1921 office building.

The new Norwich with overhead wires in place of the 'B12s', 'D16s' and 'Britannias' of the steam age.

NOTTINGHAM MR/LMS/LMR

Origins: opened 1904, Midland Railway, architect A. E. Lambert.

Location: St Pancras-Sheffield main line, junction with Derby and Lincoln lines. 126½ miles from St Pancras.

Main routes: St Pancras-Nottingham-Sheffield, Birmingham-Derby-Nottingham-Cleethorpes, East Anglia-North West, Nottingham-Skegness, and Nottingham-Manchester/Leeds/York.

Other routes: Nottingham-Beeston/Derby and Nottingham-Grantham.

Services: InterCity services St Pancras-Nottingham-Sheffield, including the 'Nottingham Executive'. Sprinter service routes: Birmingham-Cleethorpes, Nottingham-Skegness, East Anglia-Manchester/Liverpool/Blackpool, Nottingham-Manchester and Nottingham-Leeds/York. Local services to Grantham, Beeston and Derby. 197 trains daily in 1988. Fastest service to London 1 hour 43 minutes (73.5 mph), 1938 2 hours 3 minutes (61.7 mph).

Platforms: 5, including one bay; one platform out of use.

Facilities: ticket office, Travel Centre, refreshments, bookstall, parcels, left

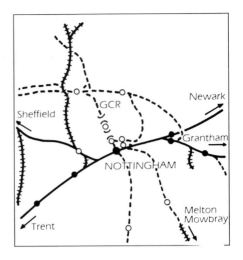

luggage, parking, car hire, city buses nearby.

Of special interest: station frontage, Area Manager's Office building opposite, former London Road station nearby.

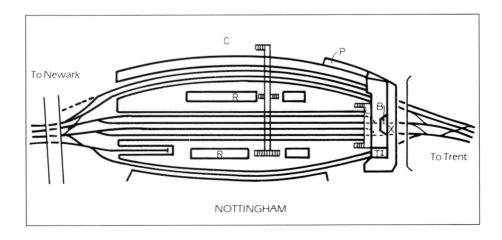

NOTTINGHAM

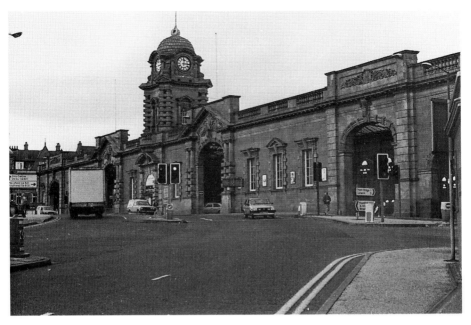

The ornate frontage designed by A. E. Lambert for the 1904 Midland Railway station at Nottingham.

Nottingham has an architecturally exciting station located in an interesting area south of the city centre, below the castle. The frontage is now in Carrington Street, but its predecessor had its entrance in Station Street which runs parallel to the present Down side parcels platform.

The Midland Counties Railway linked Nottingham with Derby from 30 May 1839, with a line to Leicester and then on to London via Rugby coming in the following year. Under the new Midland Railway, the Nottingham-Lincoln line opened in 1846, a new station in Station Street replacing the original Meadows terminus two years later. The latter then became a goods depot whose buildings now house the area manager. The 1850 Grantham-Nottingham line used the Station Street location at first but built its own station in London Road (1857) after becoming part of the Great Northern empire. After the Great Central and Great Northern's joint Victoria station opened in 1900, the Grantham trains ran on via London Road Low Level to that location until its closure in 1967. The MR opened the

Mansfield line in 1848-49, the Radford loop in 1875 and the Saxby line in 1879-80, with the GNR-backed cut-off route to Daybrook coming in 1889.

Increases in Nottingham's traffic and the threat posed by the new Victoria station prompted the Midland to rebuild in 1904. The architect, A. E. Lambert, produced a very striking building in terracotta and comprising a main block with marbled booking hall, raised roof section and office wings. In front, the *porte-cochère* facade has four ornate pedimented arches, a balustrade and a chunky central clock tower; behind, a footbridge flanked by lift shafts leads to the main island platforms. There is a Down country-end bay and an extra, now unused, platform on the Up side.

The area around Nottingham station includes a canal warehouse, train crew offices, a section of elevated GCR route and the old London Road locations. London Road Low Level, next to the canal and a parcels depot from 1944 to 1987, was built in 1857 by Thomas Hine and its chateau style is still worth savouring.

Origins: built 1847, Scottish Central Railway, architect Sir William Tite. Extended 1865, altered 1893 and 1985.

Location: intersection of Glasgow-Aberdeen and Edinburgh/Glasgow-Inverness routes. 463 miles from King's Cross.

Main routes: Glasgow-Aberdeen and Edinburgh/Glasgow-Inverness.

Other routes: Perth-Dundee/Arbroath.

Services: InterCity services to Euston/King's Cross including the sleepers 'Highland Chieftain', 'Clansman' and 'Royal Highlander'. Scotrail expresses Glasgow-Aberdeen and Edinburgh/Glasgow-Perth-Inverness, and local service to Dundee. 61 trains daily in 1988. Fastest service to London (King's Cross) 6 hours 5 minutes (76.1 mph), 1938 (to Euston) 8 hours 10 minutes (56.7 mph).

Platforms: 7, including 2 bays.

Facilities: Travel Centre, refreshments, bookstall, parcels, left luggage, car hire, parking, taxis, bus station nearby.

Of special interest: original station buildings, Station Hotel, Ritchie clock.

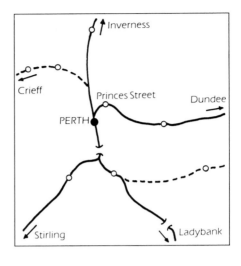

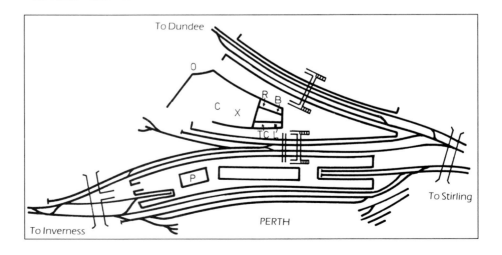

Perth, with the original main buildings on the left and the carriage sidings leading off right.

Called 'The Gateway to the Highlands', Perth has a station which is something of a railway crossroads, as well as serving the 'Fair City' itself. To the south it has routes to Glasgow and Edinburgh via Stirling and to Edinburgh over the single line to Ladybank, while northbound it has the Central Highland route to Inverness and that along the other direction of the Tay to Dundee and thence to Aberdeen. The station is not far from the town, nearer the bus station, and very near the ex-railway hotel to which it used to have direct access.

Perth station dates from 1847 and its main buildings on No 4 platform reflect the same Tudor style its architect, Sir William Tite, used at Carlisle. The north end access to the original main platform is now used for parcels traffic and the present passenger facilities are in a modern single-storey unit across the angle between the main station and the curving Dundee line platforms. Dundee trains cross the town above street level and bridge two arms of the Tay as well as passing through the now-closed Princes Street station.

The Dundee platforms are linked by a period footbridge with ramp and stairs access. Further bridges connect platforms 3 and 4, the former ending in a single line access to a group of sidings behind the hotel and recalling the volume of carriage movements that the old high-level Up Centre signal box had to handle. Its Down side equivalent can still be identified from the bay windows in the Down side main structure from which the overall roof was carried to outer walls on either side. These two-storey main buildings stand on a wide island platform and originally had a concourse on the west side. There is a double bay at the south end and a fuelling bay at the north.

The original users of Perth station became part of the Caledonian, Highland and North British systems from 1865-66 and a joint committee was formed to manage the station which was extended at that time. Subsequent alterations have produced something of a patchwork but one with a host of interesting facets ranging from the great Ritchie clock to a wealth of ironwork from Alex Findlay's works.

PLYMOUTH NORTH ROAD

Origins: opened 1877, Great Western Railway, rebuilt by BR 1960.
Location: on the former GWR West of England main line, 225¾ miles from Paddington.
Main routes: Penzance/Plymouth-Paddington. North East/South West route services via Birmingham to North East, North West and Scotland.
Other routes: Plymouth-Penzance and Plymouth-Gunnislake.
Services: InterCity services to Paddington, including sleeper service the 'Night Riviera', the 'Cornish Riviera' and 'Golden Hind Pullman'. Services over NE/SW route via Bristol and Birmingham to Leeds, York, Newcastle, Manchester and Scotland, including the 'Cornishman' and 'Cornish Scot'. Local trains to Penzance and on Gunnislake branch. 90 trains daily in 1988. Fastest service to London 2 hours 54 minutes (77.8 mph), 1938 4 hours 10 minutes (54.2 mph).
Platforms: 8, including 3 bays.
Facilities: ticket office, Travel Centre, refreshments, bookstall, parking, taxis, car hire, local buses pass nearby.
Of special interest: remains of docks routes, Royal Albert Bridge, Laira

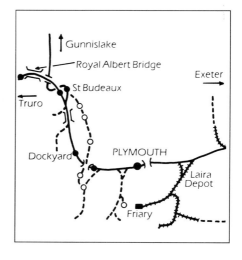

depot, scenic route to Gunnislake, South Atlantic memorial in station entrance area.

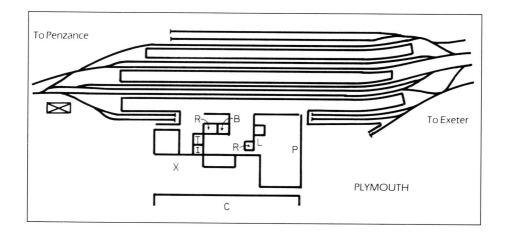

The main Down platform at Plymouth with InterCity House behind.

The trains of the South Devon Railway reached Laira on 5 May 1848 and were extended to a terminus at Plymouth Millbay the following year. This was to remain the main GWR station at Plymouth for many years, with a rail link to the docks where the Great Western's own tenders met the Atlantic liners and the nearby Duke of Cornwall Hotel opened in 1863 to accommodate their passengers. The London & South Western Railway reached Plymouth in 1876, building an Italianate terminus at Devonport and subsequently developing both its own ocean terminal and an independent access route along the Tamar from 1890. The new LSWR Friary terminus was brought into use in 1891 and was followed by a period of intense rivalry between the two railways, with the services for the liner passengers claiming a 102.3 mph speed record for the GWR in 1903 and a nasty accident three years later.

The GWR's main line was extended into Cornwall from 4 May 1859 using Brunel's impressive Royal Albert Bridge to cross the Tamar estuary and leading, in due course, to the need for a station on the present North Road site. Opened on 12 April 1877,

this replaced Millbay and Friary from 1941 and 1958 respectively and it was remodelled in its present form in 1960 using a rather functional modern style and materials.

Situated to the north of the shopping centre, BR's station at Plymouth has its principal facilities located around the entrance area on the main, Down side platform. This has double bays at each end and a subway to the two other, island platforms. InterCity House rises high above the frontage and includes the offices of the Area Manager.

Plymouth has excellent InterCity services to London and via Bristol, plus local trains on the routes to the west and serving Devonport, Dockyard, Keyham and St Budeaux. At the latter point the scenic Gunnislake branch uses the ex-SR station and passes below the main line's approach to the single line section over the Royal Albert Bridge before taking a course along the east bank of the Tamar. Traction and rolling stock maintenance and stabling for the Plymouth area takes place at the sizeable Laira depot, in a triangle created by the surviving freight branch to Friary depot.

PORTSMOUTH HARBOUR & SOUTHSEA

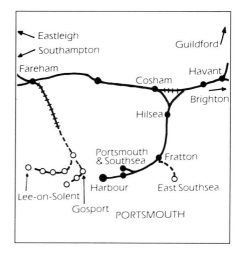

Origins: both opened 1876 (Portsmouth & Southsea on site of 1847 station), LSW and LB&SCR Joint.

Location: former LSWR and LB&SCR route from Cosham. Portsmouth & Southsea is 73¾ miles from Waterloo.

Main routes: Portsmouth Harbour to Waterloo via Guildford, to Victoria via Hove and to Cardiff via Salisbury.

Other routes: to Salisbury, Reading and Brighton.

Services: fast service to Waterloo via Guildford and semi-fasts to Victoria via Hove. All-stations services on both routes, including to Brighton, and to Southampton/Salisbury. Emus to Reading and Sprinters to Bristol and Cardiff via Salisbury. Steamer service Portsmouth Harbour-Ryde (IOW). 412 trains daily from Portsmouth Harbour in 1988 (424 from Portsmouth & Southsea). Fastest service to London 1 hour 28 minutes (50.3 mph), 1938 1 hour 34 minutes (47.1 mph).

Platforms: Portsmouth Harbour — 5, Portsmouth & Southsea — 4.

Facilities: tickets, information, refreshments, left luggage, taxis and buses at both stations. Gosport ferry from Harbour and bus to Ferryport (for France and Channel Islands), Southsea-Ryde hovercraft service link from Portsmouth & Southsea.

Of special interest: Portsmouth & Southsea — main buildings, SR trespass notice; Harbour — SR signal box, shipping activity.

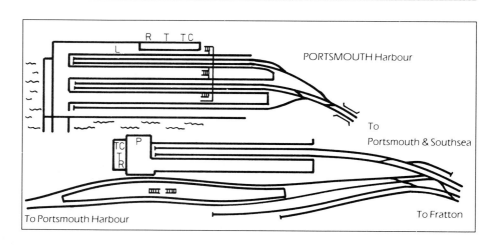

This notable maritime town, long known for its links with the Royal Navy, has two main railway stations. Portsmouth & Southsea, which serves the shopping centre area, is part terminus and part through station, the elevated course from the latter leading on to Portsmouth Harbour where the platforms project over the water to the pontoon used by the Sealink ferry to the Isle of Wight. The Gosport Ferry terminal is nearby and the Harbour station is also close to HMS *Victory* and the other historic vessels in the naval dockyard.

The first railway in the area was an 1842 branch to Gosport, but this is now closed and rail passengers use the route opened by the LB&SCR from the west on 14 June 1847. The section south from Cosham became joint with the LSWR to allow the latter's trains to work in from Fareham in the following year, although the two railways fell out again over the 'South Western' direct London route via Guildford. This opened on 24 January 1859 after a legal battle to restrain the 'Brighton' from physically blocking the line at Havant. The extension from Portsmouth & Southsea to Portsmouth Harbour dates from 2 October 1876 and at one time had wharf and dockyard branches.

In its journey across the Portsea Island part of the Portsmouth conurbation, today's railway line passes through Hilsea and then Fratton, which formerly had a branch to Southsea. Following the route of

An Up train in the high-level part of Portsmouth & Southsea station.

an earlier canal, it continues to Portsmouth & Southsea where one pair of tracks rise to the curved platforms of the high-level section, now provided with a triple-vaulted and partly glazed roof in red on a metal framework. The same remodelling scheme is providing an improved concourse with retail units at the low-level station which still retains its elaborate two-storey 1876 frontage with its ornamental ironwork, clock pediment and other decoration.

Harbour station's five platforms, equipped with water supplies for servicing the trains which turn round there, are approached via a former SR signal box. The Sealink vessels sail from the harbour end and the station offices and facilities are concentrated on the Up side platform.

Portsmouth & Southsea station showing the main frontage and the high-level through platforms.

PRESTON

Origins: opened 1880 on site of 1838 station, London & North Western and Lancashire & Yorkshire Railways, engineer William Baker.

Location: West Coast Main Line, junction with Blackburn, Blackpool and Liverpool lines. 209 miles from Euston.

Main routes: West Coast Main Line, including Euston-Blackpool; South and South West to Scotland; Manchester Victoria to Scotland; Blackpool-Preston-East Anglia; Blackpool-Preston-York; Manchester/Preston-Barrow.

Other routes: Blackpool-Preston-Colne and Blackpool-Preston-Liverpool.

Services: West Coast Main Line InterCity services Euston/Milton Keynes/Birmingham to Blackpool/Barrow/Scotland, including the 'Nightrider' and 'Night Aberdonian' (Up) sleepers and the 'Royal Scot' and 'Clansman'. Poole/Brighton/Penzance lines to Scotland, including the 'Devon', 'Wessex', 'Cornish' and 'Sussex' 'Scots'. Manchester Victoria-Preston-Scotland; Blackpool-East Anglia and Blackpool-York Sprinters. Also Blackpool South-Colne, Blackpool/Preston-Liverpool and Man-

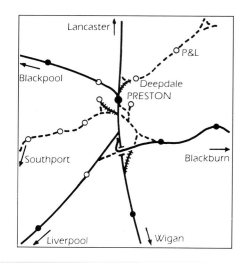

chester/Preston-Barrow services. 284 trains daily in 1988. Fastest service to London 2 hours 43 minutes (76.9 mph), 1938 3 hours 37 minutes (57.8 mph).

Platforms: 6.

Facilities: tickets and information, refreshments, bookstall, parcels, left luggage, parking, taxis, local buses nearby.

Of special interest: 1880 station buildings, 'Euston' roof, plaque, Ribble Bridge.

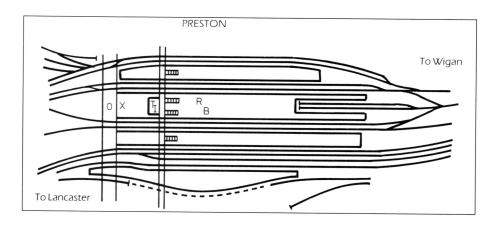

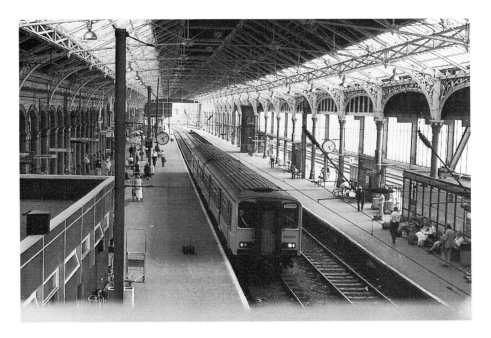

Interior of Preston station with a Class '150' Sprinter set about to depart for Barrow.

Birthplace of English Electric's well-loved 'Deltic' locomotives, Preston saw its first railway engines come into regular service in 1838, when the North Union Railway linked the town with the Liverpool & Manchester line from 31 October. Three more railways began to serve Preston from 1840, the Preston & Wyre, the Lancaster & Preston Junction and the modest Preston & Longridge, which was more concerned with carrying stone than passengers. Relationships between the four companies were less than cordial and worsened with the arrival of the Bolton & Preston Railway in 1843.

The 1838 North Union station gradually put the other Preston stations out of business, but although it was enlarged several times it was never really adequate, especially after absorbing the East Lancashire Railway's Liverpool traffic from 1849. Eventually it was rebuilt by the LNW and Lancashire & Yorkshire users in 1880 with an access from a new Fishergate Bridge to a large island platform (now numbered 3 and 4) with bays at the south end. Additional islands were added subsequently and for many years the station had a separate entrance and separate south-west platforms for trains on the Liverpool line. It also had a covered footbridge route to the Park Hotel which was designed for the LNW and LYR by Arnold Mitchell and opened in 1882.

Preston today retains its vehicular access from Fishergate Bridge which leads to the LNWR entrance building with a clock between its dormers. A paved ramp then leads on to the main 1880 platform, with footbridge access to the outer islands and to the Fishergate centre on the east side. The far Down side island is now used only for parcels and mail traffic and has not received the refurbishing accorded to the main platforms.

Preston's inverted 'vee' roof sections are good examples of standard LNWR design and are supported by an outer wall and screen and by decorated pillars. A room in the main block on the 1880 island records that it was used from 19 August 1915 to 11 November 1919 by the 'Preston Station Soldiers & Sailors Free Buffet Association' which provided refreshment and comfort to 3¼ million soldiers and sailors. In earlier times Anglo-Scottish expresses had made a 20-minute refreshment stop at Preston.

RAMSGATE

Origins: opened 1926 in place of two previous stations, Southern Railway.

Location: Kent Coast station on former SER line from Charing Cross via Ashford and ex-LC&DR route from Victoria via Faversham. 85¾ miles from Charing Cross and 79¼ from Victoria.

Main routes: Margate/Ramsgate-Charing Cross via Canterbury West and via Dover; Ramsgate-Victoria via Faversham.

Other routes: local Ramsgate-Margate service derived from above.

Services: semi-fast main line electrics to Charing Cross, joining with Dover portion at Ashford; also via Dover and running fast from Ashford. Service to Victoria via Margate and Faversham. Some trains to and from Cannon Street. 176 trains daily in 1988. Fastest service to London 1 hour 47 minutes (44.4 mph), 1938 1 hour 50 minutes (43.2 mph).

Platforms: 4.

Facilities: tickets and information, refreshments, bookstall, parcels and left luggage, parking, car hire nearby, taxis, some local buses and courtesy coach to Sally ferries.

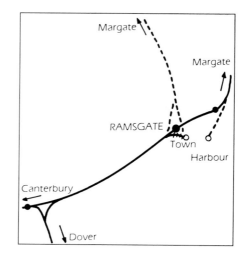

Of special interest: SR station frontage, coats of arms in booking hall; siding site of former Town station and chalk cutting access route to former Harbour station; carriage servicing depot and access movements.

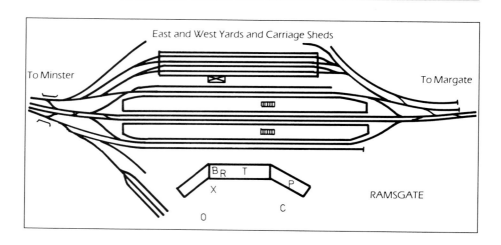

The Southern Railway's 1926 rationalization of the area provided this new station for Ramsgate.

A resort and port long favoured by leisure-seeking Londoners, Ramsgate owed some of its early popularity to its steamer links with the Thames. The first railway route to the town was that of the South Eastern Railway whose trains from Ashford reached Ramsgate Town station on 13 April 1846 and were extended on to Margate Sands on 1 December that year. Ramsgate Town was a terminal station and occupied a site on the southern, seaward side of the present location.

After having the Ramsgate traffic to itself for 17 years, the South Eastern was joined by the London, Chatham & Dover Railway on 5 October 1863 when that company arrived from Margate. The LC&DR had a station at Ramsgate Harbour, better placed than that of its rival but constricted in space and with a 1 in 75 tunnel approach. All this was altered on 2 July 1926 under a Southern Railway scheme which closed both Ramsgate stations in favour of the present one, and abandoned the old SER route to Margate for a link to that of the LC&DR. The latter's tunnel was put to use by the Ramsgate Tunnel Railway, a new

locomotive and carriage depot was built on the former triangular junction near Ramsgate Town and a new station was opened at Dumpton Park.

The 1926 station buildings at Ramsgate are on the seaward side of the line and consist of a high centre section with three great windows, then modest angled wings housing the refreshment and parcels activities. From the spacious booking hall a subway leads to the two island platforms with their administrative buildings and plain, ridged canopies. Beyond the main lines and platform loops stands the brick and wood signal box with its back to the wall of the first of the lifting, inspection and servicing sheds.

In addition to its passenger services to Charing Cross via Ashford and to Victoria over the former LC&DR route, Ramsgate is an important stock maintenance and cleaning depot and has a complement of engineering, train crew and cleaning staff. The work of the latter includes heavy cleaning on nights and mobile gangs for in-service work.

Origins: original 1840 station modified 1856, 1866-70 and 1896-99, Great Western Railway. BR remodelling 1988-89.

Location: junction of GWR main lines with SR Basingstoke and Redhill/Waterloo routes. 36 miles from Paddington.

Main routes: Paddington-Reading-West of England, Bristol and South Wales main lines, also via Oxford to Worcester, Hereford and Birmingham. South Coast via Basingstoke and via Kensington Olympia to North West, North East and Scotland.

Other routes: WR local trains on Paddington, Oxford and Westbury lines; SR routes to Waterloo, Tonbridge and via Basingstoke.

Services: InterCity services to West of England, Bristol/Weston-super-Mare and South Wales; to Worcester/Hereford/Cheltenham, and to Oxford/Banbury/Bicester/Birmingham; also ex-Poole/Brighton/Folkestone to NE/NW/Scotland and ex-Paddington to Wolverhampton/Manchester. 12 named trains, 2 sleeper services. Local trains to Paddington, Oxford and Newbury/Bedwyn and via SR to Waterloo, Guildford/Gatwick/Tonbridge and to Basingstoke/Ports

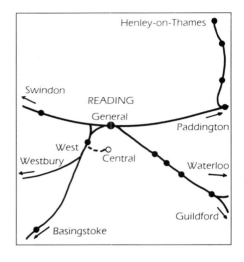

mouth. 586 trains daily in 1988. Fastest service to London 28 minutes (77.1 mph), 1938 42 minutes (51.4 mph).

Platforms: 11, including 7 bays.

Facilities: tickets and information, refreshments, bookstalls, parcels, left luggage, parking, taxis, local buses, Railair link to Heathrow airport.

Of special interest: intensive train working and new Brunel arcade.

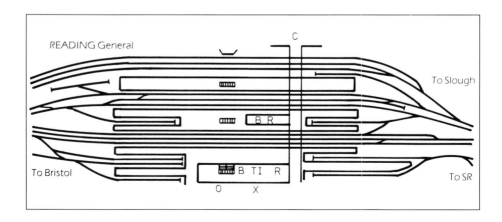

The GWR station at Reading, to be preserved within the current remodelling scheme.

Reading station serves the county town of Berkshire from a site just north of the town centre and near the Caversham Bridge crossing of the Thames. It lies on the Bristol, South Wales and West of England main lines of the Western Region and is also served by Oxford line trains, two SR routes and important north-south services via Basingstoke and via Kensington Olympia. Its 30,000 daily passengers include users of the Railair transfer link to and from Heathrow Airport and a significant volume of London commuters.

The original broad gauge main line of the Great Western Railway linked Reading with London from 30 March 1840. Brunel provided the town with one of his 'tandem' stations, with separate train sheds for arriving and departing passengers. Its operational complications increased with the addition of the Hungerford (1847) and Basingstoke (1848) traffic and a new layout replaced the previous mixture of platforms in 1856 in readiness for the opening of the line to Staines. The present buildings were added soon after.

Further changes took place at Reading around the end of the century. A remodelling of 1896-99 produced the present form of a main Down platform plus two islands in good time to handle trains on the new main line to be created via Westbury. The town also got a new goods depot branch (to Reading Central) in 1908 to help cope with its extensive freight business, which included vast quantities of biscuits from Huntley & Palmer's private siding. There was a separate, adjoining station at Reading South for SR trains until 1965 when these were moved to new platforms at the London end of the main station.

A fresh round of improvements at Reading began in 1988 with the provision of a multi-storey car park and an accompanying bridge to the Down side of the station. There, further stages of the scheme have added the new Brunel Arcade concourse and ticketing area whilst retaining the GWR two-storey frontage with its pediment and wooden clock tower behind. There is a second, elevated, two-platform station at Reading West, and the area has an extensive maintenance and servicing depot within the triangle between the two main lines.

RUGBY

Origins: opened 1886, London & North Western Railway.
Location: West Coast Main Line, junction of Northampton loop and Birmingham line with direct Trent Valley route to Stafford. 84½ miles from Euston.
Main routes: West Coast Main Line and Birmingham-Rugby-Euston.
Other routes: none.
Services: InterCity services Euston-Rugby-Manchester/Liverpool/Blackpool/Scotland/Holyhead, including the 'Irish Mail' and 'Welsh Dragon'. Midline electrics Walsall/Birmingham-Coventry-Rugby-Northampton-Euston. 87 trains daily in 1988. Fastest service to London 1 hour 4 minutes (79.2 mph), 1938 1 hour 22 minutes (62 mph).
Platforms: 8; 4, including 2 bays, in use.
Facilities: ticket and information offices, refreshments, parcels and left luggage, parking, taxis, Midland Red South buses on approach road.
Of special interest: imposing station structure, period drinking fountains, approach junctions, Avon Viaduct.

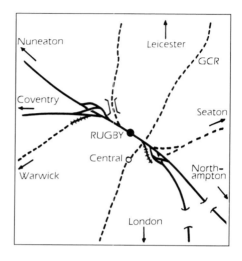

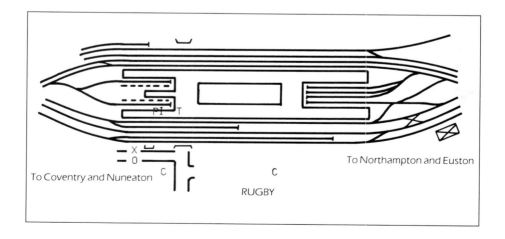

Following the opening of the London & Birmingham Railway's main line through Rugby in 1838, other areas wanting rail access to the capital helped to turn the modest market town into an important railway centre. Such lines included the 1840 Midland Counties route from Leicester and the 1850 Rugby & Stamford which also tapped the Peterborough traffic. These, with the eventual 'figure of eight' configuration of the West Coast Main Line, an LNWR branch to Leamington and the route of the Great Central's London Extension were eventually to give Rugby nine radiating lines and a significant railway industry.

Rugby's first makeshift station at Old Station Square was replaced in 1840 when the MCR completed its 11-arch Avon Viaduct to join the L&B route. Traffic growth necessitated further improvements and the LNWR duly provided a new station in 1886, essentially the one that serves Rugby today. Overpowering in the days of its great signal gantries and 25-line engine shed, Rugby now makes an interesting contrast with its neighbours at Northampton and Coventry.

From each side, Rugby is approached by two arms of the main line with flyover/under links to reduce conflicting movements. The station itself, less than half a mile from the town centre, straddles Old Mill Lane and comprises a vast island reached by subway from a modest modern entrance on the Down side. Fast through

The Down side at Rugby with the through lines passing around the station's huge island platform.

services are routed outside the island's two platform lines and it has a substantial two-storey centre block in brick and little-used bays at either end. The impression of great size is heightened by double lateral roof spans at each end and the transverse ridge and furrow glazing stretching out from the main block to substantial side walls with girder centre sections.

Rugby Central station closed in 1969 and the routes to Leamington, Peterborough and Leicester have also gone, but the 1886 station still deals with a considerable number of trains, especially on the through lines. These are signalled by the sizeable panel box on the Down side, its modern style contrasting with the GEC building at the country end of the station.

A dmu stands in one of the bays at the north end of Rugby station as a Euston-bound emu arrives.

SALISBURY

Origins: opened 1859, London & South Western Railway, architect Sir William Tite; remodelled 1900.

Location: interchange point between former LSWR main line to Exeter and the Westbury-Southampton line, 83¾ miles from Waterloo.

Main routes: Exeter-Salisbury-Waterloo; Cardiff/Bristol-Salisbury-Southampton/Portsmouth.

Other routes: Salisbury-Portsmouth.

Services: own service to Waterloo plus Exeter-Waterloo trains. Cardiff/Bristol-Southampton/Portsmouth Sprinters and all-stations and semi-fast services to Portsmouth. 104 trains daily in 1988. Fastest service to London 1 hour 26 minutes (58.6 mph), 1938 1 hour 28 minutes (57 mph).

Platforms: 6, including 2 bays; only 4 in normal use.

Facilities: tickets, information, buffet and bookstall, parcels, left luggage, car park, taxis, car hire, city buses nearby.

Of special interest: adjoining ex-GWR station, London-end water tank, 'To Call Porter' bell.

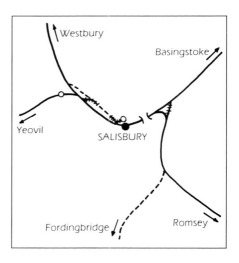

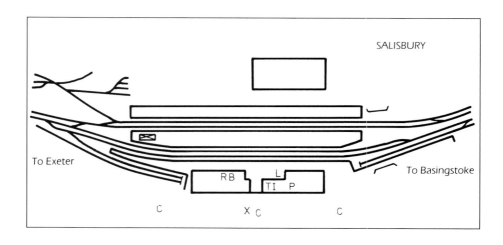

Salisbury station from the London end with the former GWR station building on the right.

The first trains to serve Salisbury arrived from Eastleigh in 1847 and used a station at Milford, on the south-east side of the city. The LSWR used the same station until 1859 when the opening of the Salisbury & Yeovil extension westwards led to a station on the present site. In a mildly Italianate style and by Sir William Tite, this consisted of a two-storey block in brick, with decorated windows and parapet, leading to a single platform used by both Up and Down trains. Beyond lay the GWR's 1856 terminus of the Wilts, Somerset & Weymouth Railway, a wooden affair with clear Brunel origins.

The first LSWR extension at Salisbury involved a separate Up platform reached by subway, but the whole layout was re-modelled in 1900 to produce the present pattern of outer platforms, central island and subsidiary platforms at each end of the main Down side complex. Executed in red brick, the new two-storey frontage block differed in style from the adjoining 1859 building and had a separate gabled entrance area with a high, glazed booking hall. With further brick buildings beneath a canopy on the island platform, the result

completely overshadowed the modest GWR terminus, where only a low wooden glazed gable and some lion masks relieved the simple brick frontage.

Both Salisbury stations adjoin Fisherton Street, about half a mile from the city centre, the active ex-LSWR complex being reached via South Western Road. The GWR trains were diverted to the SR station from 1932, the site then becoming a goods depot and retaining a period goods shed and a typical railway weighbridge for its coal business. The station buildings are still standing and exhibition trains are stabled in the yard. The SR station has a London-end extension platform for emu locals. Its facilities are concentrated on the Down side with subway access to the other main platforms, of which No 1 is now served by a through freight siding.

A bad accident at Salisbury in 1906 ended the races with the GWR over the Plymouth liner traffic, and Salisbury once had an interesting 'Salisbury Market House & Railway' local line. Although the days of the 'Atlantic Coast Express' have gone, it still accommodates steam specials from time to time.

SCARBOROUGH

Origins: opened 1845, York & North Midland Railway, architect G. T. Andrews; BR refurbishment 1988.
Location: terminus of line from York, 42 miles from that point.
Main routes: cross-Pennine route from Liverpool/Manchester.
Other routes: Scarborough-Hull.
Services: Sprinter services to Manchester via Leeds and Halifax, to Liverpool via Leeds, Huddersfield and Manchester, and to Hull. 57 trains daily in 1988. Fastest service to Liverpool 3 hours 14 minutes (43.7 mph), 1938 5 hours 6 minutes (25.2 mph).
Platforms: 5, including 2 bays.
Facilities: tickets and information, bookstall, refreshments, parcels, left luggage, parking, taxis, local buses pass.
Of special interest: main station buildings, Londesborough Road excursion station, steam excursion working turntable, Whitby line tunnel, long platform seat (capacity 100) on No 1 platform, several cliff railways on the front.

The recent award-winning improvements at Scarborough have provided the station with new ticket and

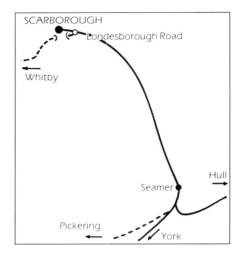

parcels offices and Travel Centre, plus a retail area which includes a buffet-cum-passenger lounge. A new glazed extension now surrounds the restored clock tower and the station has a new entrance area adjacent to the renewed 1845 wall.

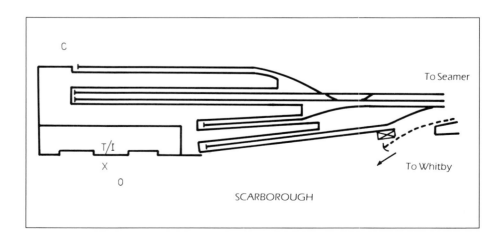

Part of the George Hudson empire, the York & North Midland Railway's line from York to Scarborough was opened on 7 July 1845, the then modest fishing port being provided with a terminal station to the designs of G. T. Andrews. This consisted of two platforms with sidings between, and a long arrival-side building in ashlar blocks, all under a typical Andrews roof. Although the station was subsequently extended by absorbing the goods shed, the extra south-side platforms have now been surrendered for development, leaving the main station area still much that of the 1845 original.

Scarborough grew as a resort as the British seaside habit developed and various alterations and extensions were made to the station that dealt with most of its visitors. The tall, unharmonious clock tower in the Baroque style was added in 1884, York-end bay platforms were provided and a separate, Londesborough Road, excursion station opened on the Down approaches in 1908. In 1934 an extra platform was created out of No 1 so that trains for the Whitby line could propel out and reverse direction at Londesborough Road through Gallows Close Tunnel and on, past the goods and locomotive depots, towards Whitby and Middlesbrough.

The original York-Scarborough railway route was followed by the line to Filey (1846) and on to Hull (1847), a single line from Pickering (1882) and then the Whitby line (1885). Only the York and Hull routes survive but these have an excellent service, including cross-Pennine Sprinters on the former. Extra holiday trains still serve Scarborough on summer Saturdays, although not in the numbers of former years

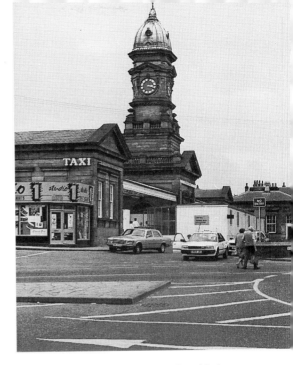

The baroque clock tower unhappily added to Scarborough's station buildings in 1884.

when thousands used the main station and the now closed Londesborough Road, and most of the four miles of stabling sidings would be needed.

Near the town and less than half a mile from the sea, Scarborough station has three main platforms plus two long bays. Access is via the long 1845 block with its end pavilions and high clock tower and with two inverted 'vee' roof spans over the area used for regular services. Towards Seamer lie the Whitby line tunnel, Falsgrave signal box and a turntable used for steam specials.

The long seat on Scarborough's excursion platform has been a boon to many a tired tripper.

SHEFFIELD

Origins: 1870 Pond Street station rebuilt 1904, Midland Railway, architect Charles Trubshaw.

Location: former Midland St Pancras-Leeds main line, junction with Retford, Doncaster, Barnsley and Manchester lines. 167 miles from St Pancras.

Main routes: Sheffield-St Pancras; North East-South West/South Wales/Poole; Sheffield-Cleethorpes/Hull; East Anglia-North West.

Other routes: Sheffield-Lincoln-Sleaford/Cleethorpes; Sheffield-Barnsley-Hundersfield/Leeds; Sheffield-York.

Services: InterCity services to St Pancras, including the 'Master Cutler', and on Newcastle/York-South West/South Wales/Poole route, including the 'Armada', 'Devonian', 'Cornishman' and 'Northumbrian'. Sprinters East Anglia-Liverpool/Blackpool, and to Hull/Cleethorpes via Doncaster. Local services to Lincoln/Sleaford/Cleethorpes, to Hundersfield/Leeds, and on Doncaster and Manchester lines. 411 trains daily in 1988. Fastest service to London 2 hours 15 minutes (74.2 mph), 1938 2 hours 52 minutes (58.2 mph).

Platforms: 9, including 4 bays.

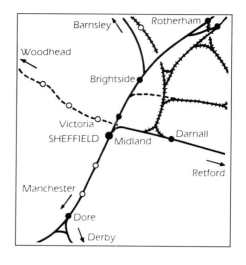

Facilities: tickets, information, refreshments, bookstall, parcels and left luggage, parking, car hire, taxis, local buses.

Of special interest: main station frontage, footbridge mural, MR tunnel portal, remains of Victoria station.

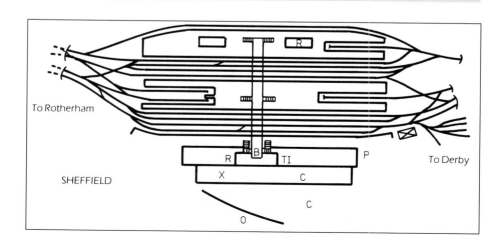

The frontage of Sheffield station showing the elegant arched arcade.

With so many trains using Sheffield station today it is difficult to imagine the city being served only by a branch line. But George Stephenson took his North Midland Railway route from Derby to Leeds around the east of Sheffield in the interests of easy gradients, and the latter's first railway was a branch to connect with the NMR at Rotherham. The Sheffield & Rotherham Railway opened from a station at Wicker in 1838 and was connected to the trunk route when it opened two years later. The next Sheffield station was a temporary one at Bridgehouses which was brought into use in 1845 with the opening of the eastern end of the Woodhead route to Manchester. Six years later Victoria station took over, growing to handle all Great Central services and the BR cross-Pennine electrics, but then closing in 1970 as a result of a rationalization of the Sheffield area railways.

The Midland Railway secured powers for a direct line from Chesterfield to Sheffield via the valley of the River Sheaf in 1864. The route opened six years later with a through station replacing the original Wicker terminus and then itself being replaced in 1904. This new station was part of a round of main-line improvements, the architect Charles Trubshaw using a warm reddish stone for the long arcaded frontage with a mixture of double and single arches and with decorative stone finials above.

The *porte-cochère* access leads to a double-domed, glazed concourse with ticketing, bookstall and refreshment facilities. Beyond this lies No 1, the main Down platform, with a double staircase access to the footbridge leading to a centre island with bays at both ends and to a further island used by Up direction services. A high retaining wall encloses the Up side, with tunnels and overbridges constricting the rail access at both ends of the layout. The station has its share of decorative ironwork, contrasting with the modern panel box on the Down side, London end.

Located near the city centre, Sheffield station is interesting for the variety of its services and the volume of interchange activity. The city also has modest stations at Brightside, Attercliffe and Darnall.

SHREWSBURY GENERAL

GWR&LNWR/
GWR&LMS/LMR

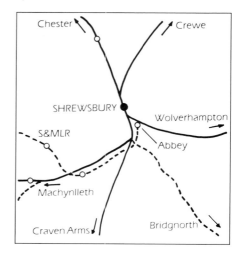

Origins: built 1848-49 for four local railways, architect T. K. Penson.

Location: junction of lines from Newport, Machynlleth, Chester, Crewe and Wolverhampton. 158 miles from Euston.

Main routes: Shrewsbury-Euston, Birmingham-Shrewsbury-Aberystwyth/Pwllheli, Cardiff-Liverpool/Manchester/North Wales, Central Wales line to Swansea.

Other routes: Shrewsbury to Crewe, Wolverhampton and Chester.

Services: InterCity service to Euston, including the 'Cambrian Coast Express' (ex-Aberystwyth); Sprinter services Cardiff-Shrewsbury-Liverpool/Manchester via Crewe, and North Wales via Chester; also on Aberystwyth and Pwllheli routes via Machynlleth. Trains to Swansea via Central Wales Line and local services to Crewe, Wolverhampton and Chester. 163 trains daily in 1988. Fastest service to London 2 hours 44 minutes (57.9 mph), 1938 (to Paddington) 3 hours 15 minutes (52.8 mph).

Platforms: 4 in use, including 2 bay platforms.

Facilities: tickets, information, refreshments and small bookstall, parcels, left luggage, car hire, taxis, some parking, buses nearby.

Of special interest: main station frontage, adjacent buildings, Severn Bridge Junction signal box, former Abbey station site, refectory pulpit of former abbey in goods yard.

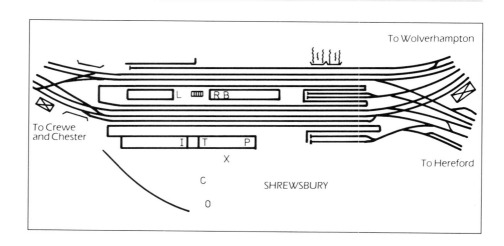

An amalgam of local railway schemes was eventually to create the 'North and West' route all the way from Newport to Birkenhead and with Shrewsbury as one of its principal junctions. It retains much of its earlier role today, acting as a gateway to Wales over the surviving route to Machynlleth and then on to the resort of Aberystwyth or north along the Cambrian Coast as far as Pwllheli.

The early railway schemes in the Shrewsbury area crystallized into lines authorized to the Shropshire Union, Shrewsbury & Birmingham, Shrewsbury & Hereford and Shrewsbury & Chester companies. Trains of the latter started using a temporary station there on 14 October 1848, the considerably grander station by T. K. Penson and Thomas Brassey coming into use in the following June. After a period of bitter in-fighting for control of the local railways, the rival Great Western and LNWR companies completed agreements for the joint control of Shrewsbury and for working arrangements in the area. Of the early lines to Shrewsbury all have survived except the GWR line from the Severn Valley and that of the Shropshire & Montgomeryshire Light Railway into Shrewsbury Abbey station.

Shrewsbury station started life as a two-storey building but was converted to three-storeys by R. E. Johnson in an impressive 1903-04 operation which supported the original building while the approach courtyard was lowered to permit the addition of

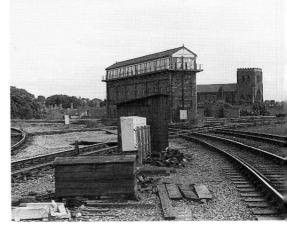

The huge, high signal box where Shrewsbury's Hereford and Wolverhampton routes separate.

a new ground floor level. The 'Tudor/Jacobean' stone building has a gabled end section and a clock tower. A battlement parapet, tall chimneys and decorated windows all add to the fine exterior from which a subway leads to the island platform. This, with its south-end bay, is now used for all services.

Near to the town centre, the station also has interesting surroundings. It bridges the River Severn and has the castle, prison and Buttermarket for companions. There are ornate gates to the right of the main station building, which has benefited from a 1984-86 joint scheme of remodelling, while the signal boxes at either end are reminders of the area's GWR and LNWR origins.

The fine station frontage at Shrewsbury, converted from two to three storeys in 1903-04.

SOUTHAMPTON CENTRAL

Origins: opened 1895 (replacing earlier station), London & South Western Railway. Rebuilt 1968, BR.

Location: former LSWR main line to Weymouth, interchange point with Portsmouth-Bristol-Cardiff route. 79¼ miles from Waterloo.

Main routes: Weymouth/Southampton-Waterloo; to the North via Reading; and Brighton/Portsmouth-Bristol-Cardiff.

Other routes: Southampton-Wareham; Portsmouth-Salisbury.

Services: Wessex Electrics Weymouth/Poole-Southampton-Waterloo, including the 'Royal Wessex'. Poole-Southampton-North West, North East and Scotland, including Edinburgh sleeper service, 'Wessex Scot' and 'Northumbrian'. Portsmouth-Cardiff Sprinters and local emu services on all four routes. 234 trains daily in 1988 (130 from Southampton Parkway). Fastest service to London 1 hour 7 minutes (70.9 mph), 1938 1 hour 30 minutes (52.8 mph).

Platforms: 4.

Facilities: ticket offices, information office, refreshments, bookstalls, parcels, left luggage, parking, taxis, car hire, local buses including service to Royal Pier for the Red Funnel route to the Isle of Wight.

Of special interest: former Terminus station, Freightliner Millbrook and Maritime terminals, dockside route to Redbridge.

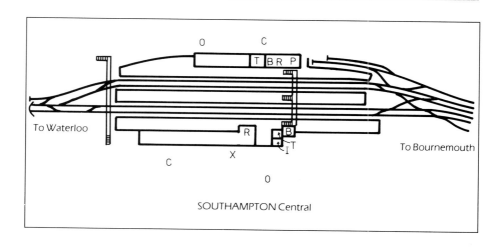

SOUTHAMPTON Central

A view of Southampton station from above the main Down side platform.

What became the main line of the LSWR and then the SR to Southampton and beyond was made up of a London & Southampton Railway project opened throughout on 11 May 1840 and the 1847 Southampton & Dorchester Railway. The former arrived along the course of the River Itchen and used a terminus in the old dock area near the Royal Pier. The latter departed along the River Test via a station that became Southampton West in 1895, was enlarged in the 1930s, and was rebuilt by BR in 1968. Southampton Terminus station closed to passengers on 5 September 1966, but the pleasant Italianate building by William Tite still exists.

The coastal line east from Southampton was added in 1866 and now all three main routes have surburban stations, Millbrook, Redbridge and Totton along the Bournemouth line, Bitterne on the Portsmouth route, and St Denys and Swaythling along the inland line. The latter, which serves the university, is followed by Southampton Parkway, the station for Southampton's airport. The Bournemouth line parallels the former SR docks which once handled the great liners and hundreds of banana and other cargo vessels. The area, although still busy, has changed in character and the railway interest is now represented by the two Freightliner terminals, Millbrook and Maritime, the latter designed specifically for the rapid clearance of sea-going containers.

The Down approach to Southampton station is through a tunnel, recently reconstructed to overcome subsidence problems caused by its canal origins. The station itself, less than half a mile from the city centre, lies between Wyndham Place and Western Esplanade and comprises outer platforms used by main-line services and the centre island which handles the local trains. The Up side has a five-storey office building and accommodates the train information office in a new section recently grafted on to the 1968 rebuilding. A similar addition has been made between the typical SR 1930s buildings on the Down side.

The main servicing activities at Southampton lie east of the tunnel, near the junction with the Eastern Docks line. West, a four-track section has connections to the Freightliner terminals as it passes behind the Western Docks.

STAFFORD

Origins: 1962 BR rebuild of 1862 London & North Western Railway station.
Location: West Coast Main Line, junction of Trent Valley and Birmingham routes. 133¼ miles from Euston.
Main routes: West Coast Main Line and Birmingham-Manchester; also South Coast to North West.
Local routes: Stafford-Stoke-Manchester, Stafford-Walsall and Stafford-Coventry.
Services: West Coast Main Line InterCity services Euston to Scotland, Lancaster/Blackpool, North Wales and Manchester/Liverpool, including the 'Merseyside Pullman', 'Welsh Dragon' and 'Irish Mail'. Liverpool-Dover and Manchester-Brighton services. Birmingham/Stafford-Manchester electrics and Stafford-Walsall locals. 124 trains daily in 1988. Fastest service to London 1 hour 35 minutes (84.3 mph), 1938 2 hours 9 minutes (62 mph).
Platforms: 6.
Facilities: ticket and information offices, refreshments, bookstall, left luggage, parcels, parking, taxis, local buses pass.

Of special interest: traffic movements including main-line freight workings, a functional station design typical of its period, concourse plaque.

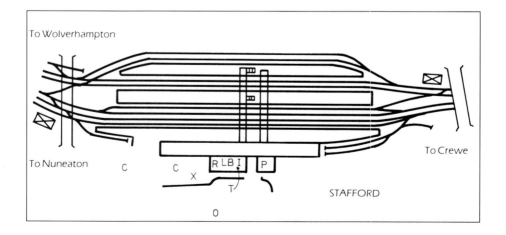

The railway importance of Stafford derives from its position at the meeting point of two arms of the West Coast Main Line, the original route from Rugby through Birmingham, and the later Trent Valley direct line via Nuneaton. The Grand Junction Railway's 1837 line from Warrington to Birmingham had a monopoly of the Stafford traffic until the newly formed LNWR company opened the Trent Valley line ten years later. Then came a line from Stafford to Wellington in 1849 and the route to Uttoxeter in 1867, this latter becoming an outpost of the Great Northern Railway but lasting only until 1939.

Above the ticket barrier on the main Up platform at Stafford a plaque reads: 'Three stations built in 1837, 1844 and 1862 precede this fourth Stafford station which was opened on Monday 31 December 1962 by the Mayor of Stafford Councillor Rees Llewellyn Tyler, a signalman at Stafford No 5 signal box and the third mayor from that box.' Despite the functional lines of the station opened by Mr Tyler, it was still a lot more attractive than the combination of mean brick entrance and long, dark platforms which were the hallmark of its predecessor.

The 1962 station consists of the main Up side platform and a high footbridge to the two islands beyond the through lines. A single-storey concourse, housing the main public facilities, projects out from the lateral administrative block which is raised to second storey height by pre-stressed

The 1962 station at Stafford, though functional, is not unattractive.

concrete uprights and horizontal support beams. Wood and decorative panels, plus an external walkway on each side, help to minimize the functional outline of this block, and a clever use of the higher lift tower and concourse projection produce a good frontal appearance. A similar situation applies to the double bridge link to the other platforms, the passenger route embracing vending and waiting areas, the latter with a good, elevated view.

The station complex stands between two overbridges with signal boxes near both, the two main line routes separating at the south end and the stub of the Wellington branch remaining in use at the north end. Like Rugby, where the two main line routes reunite, the traffic movements through Stafford are numerous and varied.

A view of the Up side of Stafford from the London-end overbridge.

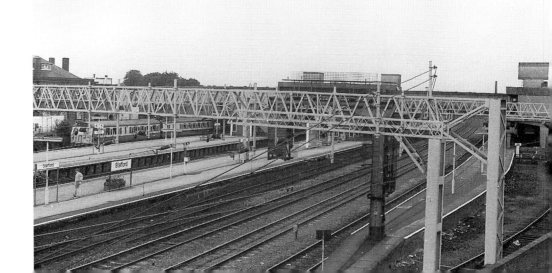

STOKE-ON-TRENT

Origins: opened 1848, North Staffordshire Railway, architect H. A. Hunt.
Location: Euston-Manchester main line, junction with Derby line. 149¾ miles from Euston.
Main routes: Manchester-Stoke-Euston, Manchester-South and South West, and Derby-North Wales.
Other routes: Manchester-Stafford and Derby-Crewe.
Services: InterCity services Manchester-Euston, including the 'Manchester Pullman', also Manchester-Paddington, Poole via Reading and Plymouth via Bristol. Manchester-Birmingham semi-fast emu services, Manchester-Stafford locals, plus Derby-Stoke-Crewe-North Wales Sprinters. 117 trains daily in 1988. Fastest service to London 1 hour 45 minutes (85.6 mph), 1938 2 hours 25 minutes (62 mph).
Platforms: 3, including one bay.
Facilities: ticket and information offices, refreshments, bookstall, parcels, left luggage, parking, taxis, PMT buses pass.
Of special interest: station building, including NSR boardroom, NSR war

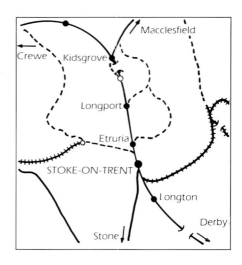

memorial, North Stafforshire Hotel opposite, The Potteries Centre shop.

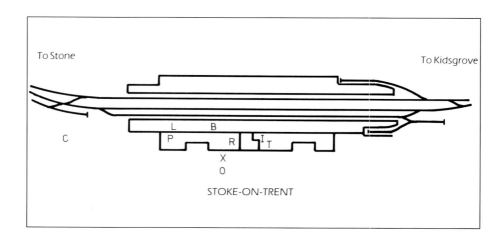

The overall roof of Stoke-on-Trent station, seen from the Up platform.

Stoke-on-Trent was the home of the well-respected North Staffordshire Railway, a locally-inspired network of semi-suburban lines conceived to meet the needs of the coal and pottery industries of the area by carrying their products and workpeople. Its emblem was the Staffordshire Knot, its nickname 'the Knotty', and the head-quarters of its 144 miles of railway and 116 miles of canal (1869) was the present station building at Stoke. Behind the boardroom window there, the NSR directors controlled their bustling local railway from its origins until the 1923 grouping.

Authorized in 1846, 'the Knotty' linked the Midland and LNWR systems with lines radiating from Stoke in five directions. The railway's principal lines were opened in 1848-49 and at one time it had ambitions for a route to London independent of its threatening LNWR neighbour but settled, instead, for the addition of more local passenger and mineral lines.

The local industrialists who founded the North Staffordshire enterprise commis-sioned a headquarters building to match its aspirations. Completed in 1850, the NSR offices were part of a wider development which created Winton Square, with the North Staffordshire Hotel opposite and railway houses on the other two sides. A bronze statue of Sir Josiah Wedgwood by Edward Davis was added in 1863 to com-plete a pleasant ensemble now mellowed by trees.

The Jacobean-style station frontage has three ornate gables and a long collonaded *porte-cochère*, over the centre of which is the mullioned bay window of the former boardroom. The end sections, also in red brick, are equally impressive, that at the north end now accommodating the Potteries Centre where the best of local products can be seen and purchased.

Inside the station a plaque commem-orates the Queen's opening of a new foyer which leads to the Up platform via a broad arch inscribed on the reverse as a memorial to NSR employees who fell in the First World War. A dark subway, partly relieved by murals, leads to the Down platform and its short bay for Manchester local services. A ridged and glazed transverse roof dating from 1893 covers the main platform area.

The Jacobean-style frontage of Stoke-on-Trent, former headquarters of the North Staffordshire Railway.

WAKEFIELD WESTGATE KIRKGATE

Origins: Westgate opened 1867, Great Northern and MS&LR railways, rebuilt BR. Kirkgate opened 1840, rebuilt by Lancashire & Yorkshire and Great Northern railways 1854-57.

Location: Westgate is on the ER London-Leeds main line, 175¾ miles from King's Cross, and Kirkgate on the ex-LYR Manchester-Normanton main line, 47¾ miles from Manchester.

Main routes: Westgate — Leeds-King's Cross.

Other routes: Westgate — Leeds-Doncaster/Scunthorpe, Leeds-Sheffield and Wakefield-Huddersfield, Kirkgate — Leeds-Barnsley-Sheffield and Westgate-Kirkgate-Huddersfield.

Services: InterCity services from Westgate to King's Cross, including the 'Bradford Executive' and 'Yorkshire Pullman'; also the 'Armada' (to Plymouth), 'Devonian' (Paignton) and 'Northumbrian' (Poole). Local trains to Leeds, Huddersfield, Doncaster/Scunthorpe and Sheffield. 166 trains daily from Westgate in 1988, 77 from Kirkgate. Fastest service to London 1 hour 56 minutes (91.1 mph), 1938 3 hours 18 minutes (53.3 mph).

Platforms: 2 at Westgate and 2 at Kirkgate.

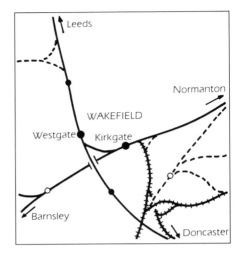

Facilities: Westgate — tickets and information, refreshments, parcels and left luggage, parking, taxis, local buses pass.

Of special interest: multi-arch Westgate approach viaduct and the sculpture 'A Light Wave' on Westgate station.

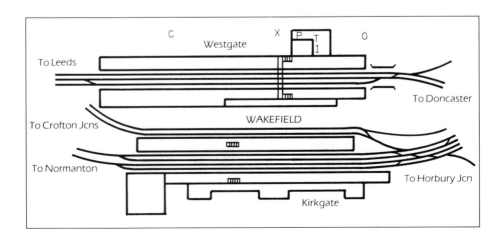

The evolving nineteenth-century railway system first catered for Wakefield with a stopping point on the 1840 North Midland line, the town then getting its own station at Kirkgate when the Manchester & Leeds Railway opened later the same year. This was used by Wakefield, Pontefract & Goole Railway (LYR) trains from 1848 and by Great Northern services from 1853. Four years later Kirkgate had been rebuilt and a spur constructed round to meet the new GN-backed line from Leeds.

Wakefield Westgate first came into use at this time, the station offices initially being accommodated in a former private house. A new station was then constructed slightly to the north. It was intended to be ready for the arrival of the West Riding & Grimsby Joint line from Doncaster, which opened in 1866, but quarrels among the prospective users delayed the opening of the new Westgate until 1 May the following year. This was a joint GNR and MS&LR location in Italianate style and with a high clock tower, and it rapidly became more important than the GNR and LYR Kirkgate station to the south of the town.

Now completely refurbished, Westgate remains Wakefield's principal station and is located near the town centre. Although comprising only two footbridge-linked platforms with an extra line between the platform lines, it has all basic facilities and handles a substantial number of trains, including the Leeds-London InterCity service. Contrasting with the modern Up-

A Leeds-bound Sprinter calls at the Down platform at Wakefield Westgate.

side entrance, the red brick buildings and exterior wall on the Down side betray the station's GNR origins. It has an interesting light sculpture created in wood in the former Down bay area at the Leeds end.

Further from the centre of Wakefield and with a few facilities, Kirkgate retains its 1857 main building with a long stone frontage where two-storey conventional offices are linked by a facade with a decorative centre section entrance. There is a subway to the Up island where the wall of the erstwhile overall roof survives. The civil engineer uses a former goods area at the east end of Kirkgate and Westgate has an active vehicle traffic dock and compound at the north end.

The imposing frontage of the 1857 Great Northern and LYR station at Wakefield Kirkgate.

WARRINGTON BANK QUAY CENTRAL

LNWR/LMS/LMR
CLC/LMR

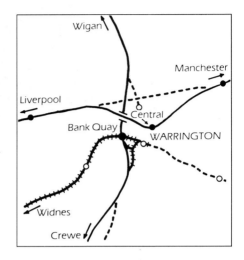

Origins: Bank Quay opened 1868, London & North Western Railway; Central opened 1873, Cheshire Lines Committee.

Location: Bank Quay is on the West Coast Main Line, 182 miles from Euston, and Central on the Manchester-Liverpool line, 18½ miles from Lime Street.

Main routes: Bank Quay — West Coast Main Line plus South/South West-Scotland via Birmingham. Cross-Pennine route Hull/Leeds-Chester/North Wales. Central — Liverpool-East Anglia and Manchester-Liverpool.

Other routes: Manchester (Oxford Road)-Central-Hunts Cross.

Services: Bank Quay — InterCity services on the West Coast Main Line including Euston-Blackpool/Stranraer, sleepers to Euston and the 'Lancashire Pullman'. Plymouth/Poole/Brighton route services via Bristol and Reading to Scotland, including the 'Devon', 'Wessex', 'Cornish' and 'Sussex' 'Scots'. Cross-Pennine Sprinters Hull/Leeds-Chester/North Wales. Central — Yarmouth/Norwich-Liverpool Sprinters and Manchester/Oxford Road-Central-Hunts Cross/Liverpool service. Daily services in 1988: Bank Quay — 78; Central — 104. Fastest service to London 2 hours 17 minutes (64.3 mph), 1938 3 hours 23 minutes (53.8 mph).

Facilities: Bank Quay — tickets and information, refreshments and bookstall, parcels and left luggage, parking, taxis, buses pass. Central — ticket office, bookstall, parking, local buses.

Of special interest: freight workings through Bank Quay, buildings (including former CLC warehouse) at Central.

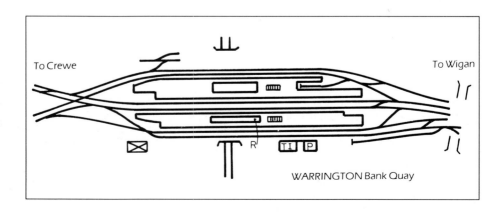

WARRINGTON Bank Quay

Industrial background at Warrington Bank Quay as a West Coast Main Line train draws into the Up platform.

Like Wigan, to the north, Warrington has two contrasting stations. Bank Quay on the West Coast Main Line is a BR rebuild, but Central, on the Manchester-Liverpool route of the old Cheshire Lines Committee, is every inch a traditional railway station despite some modest BR improvements. A third station, Bank Quay 'Low Level', closed on 9 September 1963, although part of its Merseyside route remains open for freight.

Trains came early to Warrington in the shape of an 1831 branch from the Liverpool & Manchester Railway to Dallam Lane, but the station there was closed six years later in favour of a new one on the Grand Junction line to Birmingham. It too closed, in 1868, in favour of the Bank Quay site where the present modest station is typical of the earlier BR rebuilds and takes the same pattern as that at Wigan, viz single-storey entrance building with subway access to two island platforms at a higher level. The Widnes line passes below, but Bank Quay no longer deals with the Manchester/Liverpool trains that used to call at its lower platforms.

The ex-CLC station at Warrington lies on what was formerly a loop from the direct Manchester-Liverpool route and was opened on 1 August 1873. It comprises two long platforms which follow an overbridge and are filled with the aura of bygone railways. The main buildings are on the north side, a long stone block with supplementary pedimented entrance, but today's passengers use the stairs at the town end where a modest, but pleasant, entrance arcade has been created. This houses the station's ticket office and a small bookstall. East of Central's platforms stands a great brick warehouse, still proclaiming its 'Cheshire Lines' ancestry.

South of Bank Quay, the West Coast Main Line crosses first the River Mersey and then the Manchester Ship Canal. Between the station and the river, Warrington Yard stands on the Up side, part of the route used for exchanging traffic with the Widnes line, and with a connection to the nearby traction depot. A considerable volume of oil, coal and other bulk freight movements take place in and around the Bank Quay area.

The great elevated Warrington Central station with the new entrance area alongside the road.

WIGAN
NORTH WESTERN WALLGATE

LNWR/LMS/LMR
LYR/LMS/LMR

Origins: North Western — LNWR station of 1888, rebuilt by BR. Wallgate — new station by LYR 1896.

Location: North Western — West Coast Main Line, just north of junction with St Helens line, 193¾ miles from Euston. Wallgate — on the Southport/Kirkby-Manchester Victoria line.

Main routes: North Western — WCML and Liverpool-Preston/Blackpool. Wallgate — Manchester Victoria-Southport/Kirkby.

Other routes: Liverpool-Wigan North Western.

Services: North Western — InterCity services, including the 'Lancashire Pullman', from Euston/Coventry/Birmingham to Lancashire, Cumbria and Scotland, and South/South West-Scotland including the 'Wessex Scot' and 'Cornish Scot'. Local trains to Liverpool and Preston/Blackpool. Wallgate — trains to Manchester, Bolton, Southport and Kirkby. North Western 103 trains daily in 1988, Wallgate 90. Fastest service to London 2 hours 29 minutes (78.1 mph), 1938 3 hours 46 minutes (51.4 mph).

Platforms: North Western — 6, including 2 bays; Wallgate — 3, including one bay.

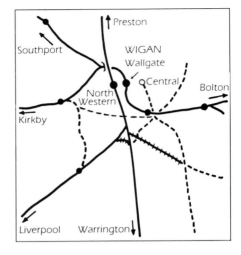

Facilities: North Western — tickets, information, refreshments and bookstall, parcels and left luggage, parking, taxis, local buses. Wallgate — tickets, bookstall, local buses.

Of special interest: modern and period station contrast, Wallgate hoist and period notice; Wigan Pier half a mile away.

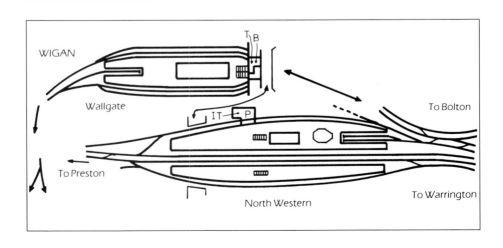

The 1896 station built by the Lancashire & Yorkshire Railway at Wigan Wallgate.

The Great Central Railway served Wigan from Manchester but the former's Central station closed on 2 November 1964 leaving the town with its two present stations, North Western on the West Coast Main Line and Wallgate on the former Lancashire & Yorkshire Railway line. The two lie close together, near the town centre, and make an interesting contrast in styles, the main-line station having been pleasantly modernized and Wallgate retaining its nineteenth-century form.

Wigan's coal traffic put it on the early railway map with a branch from the Liverpool & Manchester Railway opening to Chapel Lane on 3 September 1832. Six years later the town got a new station when the embryo main line was completed to Preston, a short Springs Branch opening at the same time. The 1838 station then lasted for 50 years until the one now remodelled was built. Wallgate station dates from 2 February 1896 but is the third one on the former LYR system which first reached Wigan in 1848.

Wigan's North Western station has a small entrance complex in red brick housing ticket and information offices with a parcels office at the rear. A subway then leads to the two island platforms, the Up one housing a buffet-cum-bookstall and a rather unusual multi-sided wooden waiting shelter. The basic layout is reversed at Wallgate where the two-storey red brick office block with projecting canopy stands at street level. Ticket office, bookstall and hoist then precede the wide stairs down to the island platform with its bay at the Southport end.

A West Coast Main Line Down train draws into Wigan North Western.

WINDSOR CENTRAL RIVERSIDE

GWR/GWR/WR
LSWR/SR/SR

Origins: Central opened 1897 on site of 1849 station, Great Western Railway. Riverside opened 1849, London & South Western Railway, architect Sir William Tite.

Location: Central is the terminus of a branch from Slough (WR), 20¾ miles from Paddington, and Riverside the terminus of a branch from Staines (SR), 25¾ miles from Waterloo.

Main routes: Riverside-Waterloo.

Other routes: Central-Slough.

Services: half-hourly emu service Riverside to Waterloo and half-hourly dmu service Central to Slough; extra trains in the peaks. 86 trains daily from Central in 1988, 71 from Riverside. Fastest service to London (Paddington) 32 minutes (38.9 mph), to Waterloo 47 minutes (32.8 mph); 1938 33 minutes (37.7 mph) and 47 minutes (32.8 mph) respectively.

Platforms: Central — 1; Riverside — 3.

Facilities: Central — tickets and information, refreshments, left luggage, parking, taxis, local buses. Riverside — tickets and information, parcels and left luggage, parking.

Of special interest: architecture and royal influence at both stations, Royalty & Empire exhibition at Central, bowstring Brunel bridge on approach to Central, and entrance gates there; Thames and steamers near Riverside.

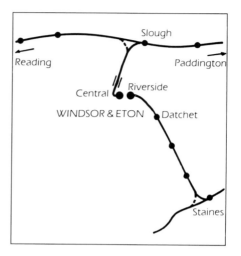

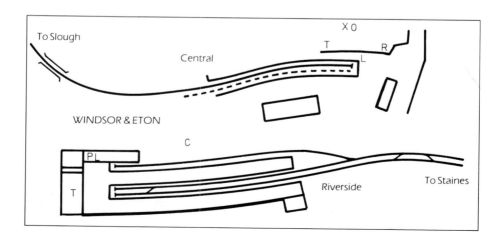

Both the Great Western and London & South Western railway companies wanted to serve the royal Windsor township, but neither Windsor Castle nor Eton College were quite as keen, the latter clearly seeing railways as a major escape temptation for its less dedicated pupils. In the end both concerns achieved their ambition after making an assortment of concessions, the GWR branch from Slough reaching Windsor on 8 October 1849 and the LSWR line from Staines being completed on 1 December of that year.

Windsor still has its two stations. The ex-GWR one, served by a multiple unit shuttle service from Slough, is Windsor & Eton Central and the three-line, ex-LSWR terminus, with its own service of emus to Waterloo, is Windsor & Eton Riverside. Both are conveniently situated and warrant their suffixes, and both have a number of distinctive features reflecting their status as 'royal' stations.

Central station is served by a single line which crosses the Thames by a Brunel wrought iron, single-span bowstring bridge to reach the long station platform at the end of which stands a turreted brick office block. The entrance roadway is marked by a combination of arch and decorated screen which spans the whole access and bears the rebuilding date of 1897. Separate covered routes then lead to the platform and to the royal waiting rooms, now embodied in a Tussaud's ex-

The elegant entrance to Windsor & Eton Central, still with the GWR legend and coat of arms.

hibition complex entitled 'Royalty and Railways'.

Riverside station's Tudor style is quite different from the French leanings of Central. It is a much more compact place, but curiously pleasing with large mullioned windows for the booking hall and separate entrances for carriage and foot passengers on either side. Blue engineer's bricks are used to decorate the outer wall, the decoration including royal initials and monograms and also those of the architect William Tite and of LSWR officials of the day. This wall is pierced by 14 entrances formerly used for cavalry access, and a separate building at its far end was formerly the royal waiting room. The latter is topped by a weather vane and has its own entrance from the road plus separate access to the platform behind.

A Waterloo train stands at Windsor & Eton Riverside. The entrance door to the former royal waiting rooms is on the left.

WOLVERHAMPTON HIGH LEVEL LNWR/LMS/LMR

Origins: rebuilt by BR on site of 1853 High Level station, London & North Western Railway.

Location: West Coast Main Line via Birmingham, junction with Shrewsbury line. 128 miles from Euston.

Main routes: West Coast Main Line, Scotland/North West-South West/ South Coast, Euston/Birmingham-Shrewsbury/Mid Wales.

Other routes: Stafford/Wolverhampton-Walsall and Birmingham-Shrewsbury.

Services: West Coast Main Line InterCity services to North West and Scotland, and to Euston. Scotland/ North West to South West via Bristol and South Coast via Reading, including the 'Sussex', 'Wessex' and 'Devon' 'Scots'. Euston-Birmingham-Wolverhampton-Shrewsbury-Aberystwyth/ Pwllheli, including the 'Cambrian Coast Express'. Local services Stafford/ Wolverhampton-Walsall and Birmingham-Wolverhampton-Shrewsbury. 217 trains daily in 1988. Fastest service to London 1 hour 54 minutes (67.4 mph), 1938 2 hours (64 mph).

Platforms: 4, including one bay.

Facilities: ticket and information offices, refreshments, bookstall,

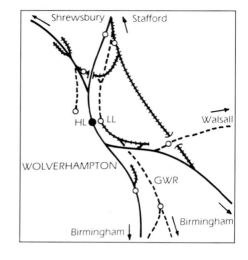

parcels and left luggage, multi-storey car park, taxis, West Midlands bus station nearby.

Of special interest: former GWR Low Level station, canal and warehouse, LNWR war memorial, Railfreight steel terminal.

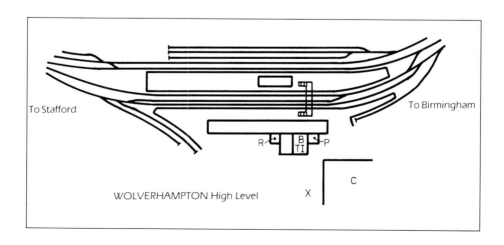

WOLVERHAMPTON High Level

Looking down on the former High Level station at Wolverhampton with the Shrewsbury bay on the left.

The view from the multi-storey car park outside Wolverhampton station reproduced here reveals something of the town's turbulent railway history. In the distance is the great brick goods depot at Wednesfield Heath, marking the route taken by the Grand Junction Railway when it opened its early line from Birmingham to Warrington on 4 July 1837. This was not close enough to Wolverhampton proper to satisfy the town's railway ambitions and its traffic was subsequently fought over by rival railways for nearly 20 years. To the right and below stood the long frontage, in blue engineering bricks, of the GWR's Low Level station, closed since 1972 in favour of the modern station on the High Level site of its LNWR rival. A subsidiary platform at the latter recalls the struggles of the Shrewsbury & Birmingham Railway, and the adjacent canal is a reminder of past altercations over transhipment traffic.

The 1837 GJR line was followed by an 1849 line from Shrewsbury to a terminus near the present site and an LNWR route from Birmingham via Tipton to Bushbury in 1852, the LNWR then showing con-siderable reluctance to complete a joint Wolverhampton Queen Street station. In 1853 the Oxford, Worcester & Wolverhampton Railway approached from Stourbridge and in 1854 the GWR (BW&DR) arrived from Birmingham, that year also producing a link up of the various systems and the opening of the GWR/OW&W Low Level station. From this time onwards the old rivalries diminished and were only briefly called to mind when the BR rationalization of passenger services in the area closed the Low Level station in favour of rebuilding its old High Level rival.

Today's Wolverhampton station, approached from the town and bus station by a landscaped route over the canal, has its main facilities in a projecting arm of the Down side buildings. There is a brass LNWR war memorial plaque on the Down platform which has a bay for parcels and mail at one end and a curving platform for Shrewsbury trains at the other, the latter with a 13 milepost opposite. A covered footbridge leads to the Up side island where the modern signal box stands beyond the London end, opposite a large mill complex.

Origins: built 1871-77, North Eastern Railway, architect Thomas Prosser.

Location: East Coast Main Line, junction with Scarborough and Harrogate lines. 188½ miles from King's Cross.

Main routes: East Coast Main Line; North East-South West/South Wales/South Coast; Newcastle-York-Liverpool; Scarborough-York-Leeds-Manchester/Liverpool.

Other routes: York-Scarborough; York-Darlington/Newcastle; York-Selby/Hull; York-Doncaster; York-Sheffield; York-Harrogate-Leeds; York-Hebden Bridge/Manchester.

Services: InterCity services between London and Newcastle and Scotland including the 'Talisman', 'Flying Scotsman', 'Highland Chieftain', 'Aberdonian', 'Cleveland Executive' and 'Tees-Tyne Pullman'; also on the North East-South West route via Birmingham including the 'Armada', 'Devon Scot' and 'Cornishman', to Cardiff, and the 'Northumbrian' to Poole. Newcastle-York-Liverpool services. Cross-Pennine Sprinters Scarborough/York-Leeds-Manchester-Liverpool via Huddersfield, and to Hebden Bridge/Manchester via Bradford. Local services to Doncaster, Selby, Hull, Sheffield, Harrogate/Leeds and Darlington/Newcastle. 243 trains daily in 1988. Fastest service to London 2 hours 2 minutes (92.7 mph), 1938 3 hours (62.8 mph).

Platforms: 10, including 5 bays.

Facilities: ticket office and Travel Centre, information point, refreshments, bookstall, parcels, left luggage, car hire, parking, taxis, local buses, coach tour starting point.

Of special interest: station frontage, hotel and tea room buildings; decorative ironwork, clock, plaques, NER tile map and ex-Haxby NER signal. Also National Railway Museum, ER headquarters building, old station and NER war memorial.

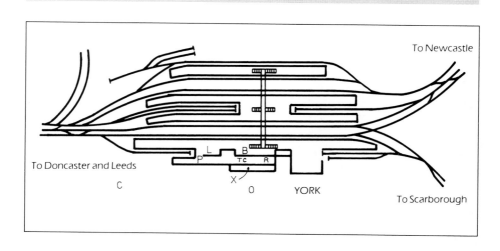

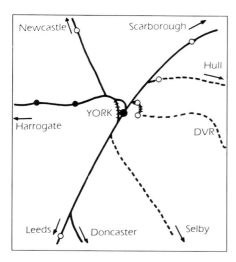

Ancient Roman and Viking stronghold, great cathedral city, target of early railway promoters and power base of George Hudson, 'The Railway King', York remains a fine city and an important railway centre. The old North Eastern Railway made its headquarters there, with BR's North Eastern and then Eastern Region following suit, and York is the home of Britain's premier collection of railway history, housed at the National Railway Museum in Leeman Road. The station is an impressive one and although the layout has been simplified recently, as part of the works complementing the electrification of the East Coast Main Line, it still deals with a significant volume of main-line, North East/South West, cross-Pennine and local services.

The Hudson-dominated York & North Midland Railway obtained its Act of Parliament in 1836 and on 30 May 1839 began operation, using a temporary station near Queen Street Bridge at York. Two years later York had been linked with London via Birmingham and the Great North of England Railway was pushing north towards Darlington. It reached there in 1841, the year in which a permanent station was brought into use at York, a three-platform affair at Tanner Row, just inside the city walls. The site is now used for parking but the access arch and part of the platform area can still be seen.

More lines were opened from York later in the 1840s, to Scarborough in 1845, to Market Weighton and to Knaresborough in 1847 and then, in 1850, it obtained direct access to London via the new Doncaster-King's Cross main line of the Great Northern Railway. This was shortened in 1871 by the opening of a link through Selby, and in the same year work was started on the present station at York which was to be opened on 25 June 1877, with the adjoining hotel being completed the following year.

York's new station was designed by Thomas Prosser but influenced by Newcastle and Paddington and by his successors as NER architect Benjamin

The main platforms at York prior to remodelling, with the Scarborough lines veering off to the right.

The interior of York station showing the footbridge, former signal box, roof details and a NE/SW HST.

Burleigh and William Peachey. The frontage faces the city walls and comprises the nine-arch portico, a delightful tea room building added by William Bell in 1906, a secondary entrance, and then the three-storey hotel block with balustraded attic section and tall chimneys at each corner. Behind the station portico there is an un-distinguished and largely hidden adminis-tration block, then the dramatic four arches

of the roof which covers an area 800 ft long and 234 ft wide. The largest span stretches for 81 ft across the through lines and all the spans have end screens and decorated columns to support the wrought iron ribs of the glazed roof area.

Within the station there is a concourse area whose centrepiece is a former NER signal from Haxby. A York Civic Trust plaque records that the station was, on

The portico outside York station with the former railway hotel and sightseeing tour coaches.

A secondary entrance at York between the hotel and the 1906 tea room building just visible on the left.

opening 'said to be the largest station in the world'. A second circulating area houses further facilities including the traditional style bookstall, and it has an excellent example of one of the NER's system maps executed in tiles on the station wall. A footbridge of generous proportions and with advertisements in the riser sections leads, via the former signal box and the huge decorated clock, to the outer platforms.

The new layout at York gives it single bays at each end of the main Up side platform, where six bays were needed in the days when six different railways worked into York. The Down side island has three bay platforms instead of four and the number of through lines has been cut from eight to five.

Among the many interesting features of York station is a dedication on the Up side waiting room to Station Foreman William Milner who died in 1942 and who was posthumously awarded the King's Commendation. A keen member of the LNER First Aid Movement, Milner 'gave his life in an attempt to gain a box of medical supplies urgently needed for treating air raid casualties. He entered a blazing building near this (waiting room) site at the height of the attack on 29 April 1942 which caused extensive damage to the station. When his body was found he was still holding the box of first aid equipment'.

In addition to the main station, York had two stations on the Foss Islands branch, one for Rowntree employees and the other the headquarters of the Derwent Valley Light Railway. The 1906 NER/ER headquarters offices have a variety of well-combined architectural styles and the NER war memorial by Sir Edwin Lutyens, in Leeman Road, is another facet of the high railway interest of the York area.

Jowett's Railway Atlas

of Great Britain and Ireland
by Alan Jowett
Foreword by David Shepherd OBE FRSA

Provides a complete record of all railways in existence during the first two decades of the present century, together with subsequent additions up to the mid 1980s. 150 pages of maps, 7,500-entry index.

'. . . a great boon for settling arguments'
Sunday Telegraph

'Such a beautiful atlas . . . is a work of art in itself' David Shepherd

'. . . a magnificent achievement. I think it's wonderful' Miles Kington

PSL Field Guides

by Geoffrey Body

This series, so far covering the entire Western, Southern, Eastern and Anglia regions of British Rail, provides a unique and wide-ranging picture of our railway network, embracing not only the operation and hardware of a modern railway system, but also its historical origins and special features.

Gazetteer detailing all important locations
● maps and photos ● services and traffic
● civil engineering features ● preservation

Railways of the Western Region
Railways of the Southern Region
Railways of the Eastern Region
    Vol 1: Southern operating area
    Vol 2: Northern operating area

Encyclopaedia of British Railway Companies

by Christopher Awdry

In this remarkable Encyclopaedia, Christopher Awdry gives details of over 1,000 British railway companies which opened at least part of their projected lines, be it a few hundred yards or many hundreds of miles.

Information on the route and purpose, the promoters and the dates of authorization, building, opening, amalgamation or closure are supported by unique 'family trees' showing how every company, by acquisition, absorption or merger, found its way into the 'Big Four' of 1923 or the London Passenger Transport Board, or, in some cases, retained independence to the end.

It is the definitive work on the subject, and an invaluable reference source for every railway enthusiast, historian and researcher.